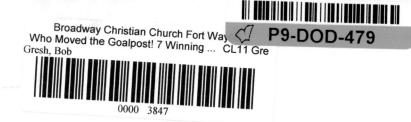

Bob has written an engaging and practical tool for young men to use in avoiding the deadly trap of sexual bondage and addiction. Revival will never be able to come to our land if the church doesn't rise up and begin to effectively address this issue. So let the fire fall and let it start with the next generation!

Dr. Ted Roberts, Pastor and author of Pure Desire

Finally we have a hard-hitting Christian book on the secret issues guys deal with. Every guy I work with on campus is facing the warfare of lust. This book gives a practical, step-by-step game plan for victory.

Doug Williams, Pen State University Campus Minister

I've read every book I can find on the subject and was always left with a hunger for the next one, hoping it might have the answers. I've finally found them in *Who Moved the Goalpost?* There's nothing like this out there.

Tony, 19 years old

This book is unique . . . different from any sexual purity book I've read. I put the majority of those on the shelf after reading the first paragraph and surmising that the person writing it was in no position to tell me about my libido, because he obviously didn't possess one himself. This book is amazingly easy to read!

Don, Youth Pastor

Who Moved the Goalpost?

BOB GRESH

MOODY PRESS
CHICAGO

Book Design by Julia Ryan

Library of Congress Cataloging-in-Publication Data

Gresh, Bob
Who moved the goalpost? / Bob Gresh.
p. cm.
Includes bibliographical references.
ISBN 0-8024-8331-3
1. Young men–Religious life. 2. Sex–Religious aspects–Christianity. I. Title.

BV4541.3 .G74 2001
241'.66–dc21

2001030738

1 3 5 7 9 10 8 6 4 2

Printed in the United States of America

TO ROBBY

Stand tall on my shoulders
and honor the blessing.

Be strong and brave.
God is with you
wherever you go.

JOSHUA 1:9

Acknowledgments

A special thanks to all those who pushed, pulled and dragged me into completing this book.

To Deb Haffey and Tippy Duncan for continually encouraging me and being patient with me even when my face was nose-deep in the goalpost.

To my graphic designers Julia Ryan, Andy Mylin and Andy Heckathorne for lending a nerd a little bit of "cool."

To Bill Thrasher, Greg Thornton, Dennis Shere, Dave DeWit, and Jim Vincent for their uncompromised commitment to keeping the focus on sharing Christ through books.

To my pastors David Janssen, Pete Cannizzaro, and Jonathan Weibel, who remind me of those three poor guys in the front lines of the revolutionary war. One carries the flag, one beats the drum, and one plays the flute. They inspire me by walking in front.

To Doug Williams for believing in the vision.

To Dan, Kay and Darin, my in-laws by chance, my family by heart.

To Robby and Lexi for sharing your time and for blessing each day of my life.

To my mom. The quality of your heart humbles me.

To my wife Dannah, my Proverbs 31 woman, for reading my mind and writing my book. I thank God that I get to come home to you.

CONTENTS

The Pregame

CHAPTER 1

who Moved the goalpost?

I did. And you can too

> **[God's grace] teaches us to say "No"** to ungodliness and worldly passions, and to live self-controlled, upright and godly lives in this present age, while we wait for the blessed hope—the glorious appearing of our great God and Savior, Jesus Christ.
>
> TITUS 2:12–13

who Moved the goalpost? I did. And you can too

It's funny the things a guy remembers.

I stood facing the aisle waiting for the organ to cue my entrance into the church sanctuary. Two hundred guests were craning their necks to get a look at me and my groomsmen. I was agitated and nervous. It had nothing to do with the fact that I'd be at the altar of my own wedding ceremony in moments. It was the fight erupting behind me.

"Jamie, don't be stupid," insisted Troy VanLiere. "Those are my shoes, and you know it."

"If they are your shoes, why are they on my feet?" Jamie Meiden teased.

"You tick me off," growled Troy.

I looked around to see Jamie grinning.

"Great! That's just great!" I grumbled. "*What* are you guys arguing about now?"

I shouldn't have asked that. It just started the whole thing over for about the tenth time. Somehow the tuxedo shop had mixed up our shoe order, and Troy's toes were painfully crammed into his. It was a familiar thing to hear these two argue. After living together for a year, it was common for all three of us to brawl it out. In the end it always worked out, but it was my wedding day and I didn't feel like waiting for things to run their course.

"Sorry, Bob," they both said, secretly laughing at my nervousness.

The next several hours were a blur.

Soon, I was on my way to my honeymoon suite in Baltimore. It would be a very looooong four-hour trip. After being carted around in antique cars, escorted into a waiting crowd by a live orchestra and dining on filet and shrimp, Dannah and I sat in my economy car in jeans and T-shirts listening to a cheap radio. We talked as we drove. We'd talked like this hundreds of times. It was surreal. We were married, but nothing really felt different. As normal as it all felt, I realized my start-stop, start-stop driving was reflecting an inner conflict.

45 to 60 in 6 seconds.

. . . . 60 to 25 in 5 seconds.

. . . . . . 25 to 70 in 7 seconds.

70 to 40 in 4 seconds.

As my mind reeled with delightful thoughts of "I can! We can! We're gonna!" I found myself accelerating. Then I remembered that just a few hours earlier I had joked with my buddies that I would not have sex tonight. They'd been teasing me, saying, "We know what you'll be up to tonight." I wanted to "one-up" them, so I just thought we'd wait a few days so they could not, would not know!

It was hard to believe that I was actually allowed to have sex now, but I was. My new bride sat next to me in the pink button-down shirt that had driven me nuts for months. It was as modest as they come, but somehow . . . wow! The smell of my favorite perfume invited me closer.

There would be no waiting.

The waiting was over.

For four hours, I planned, sweated, accelerated, coasted, and hit the brakes as I tried to figure it all out. Who was going to undress first? How would it all work out? What would I say?

What a ride!

At the honeymoon suite, Dannah went into the bathroom. Six hours and forty-two minutes later—OK, maybe it was only fifteen minutes—she emerged. The thought occurred to me that I'd always worried that I'd end up marrying someone ugly, but when she came out I realized, "She's the one that did!" But she didn't seem to know. Who was I to break the news?

She was the girl I'd always dreamed about. Her blond hair fell in loose curls around her shoulders. Her white and pink silk pj's glistened in the low lights. She looked like an angel.

she was simply spectacular

She was simply spectacular.

What happened next was nothing short of sacred. It was a holy thing.

←-------✕✕✕✕-O-O-O-O-------→

Somehow, I had muddled my way through the temptation and managed to be a virgin until my wedding night. Guess those guys were right. I couldn't wait past that first night. But you know what? It was worth waiting *until* that night!

How did I make it till that night? God knows that I was not perfect. I marvel at NBA wonder A. C. Green. He's been described in *Sports Illustrated* as "achingly handsome, drippingly rich and gallantly polite. Yet, at thirty-six, he swears he has never, not once, gotten busy."[1] How's a guy like that fend off all the women begging him for attention in the midst of the sexual playpen surrounding professional sports. I cannot wrap my ever-tempted mind around that.

. . . bammm!

Over the past few years I've seen quite a few sports videos featuring sport's greatest bloops and blunders. Invariably, you'll see a classic video clip of some guy heading into the end zone to catch a pass or to tackle someone when . . . bammm! He smashes face first into the goalpost. Until 1974, the NFL's field goalpost was right on the goal line instead of at the back of the end zone as it is today. This kind of scene happened again and again over the years until someone had a great idea—to move the goalpost out of the way. Problem solved.

Sometimes when you're in the game of life rushing around on the field, the excitement distracts you and the next thing you know you're nose deep in the goalpost of lust. You knew where the goalpost was and you knew how hard it was and that it hurt when you hit it. But what do you do . . . start playing all over again and of course . . . bammm!

I'd like to teach you strategies that can separate you from the constant crash of that goalpost of lust.

Who moved the goalpost?
I did.
And you can, too!

Many of us have moved along in the current of the pop culture. We find ourselves doing what's "normal." We go to movies with foul language and nudity. We watch the most popular (and funniest) TV shows that are filled with sexual jokes. We're exposed to ads featuring barely clothed women who lure us to buy clothing, cars, food, and music. Eventually we plow into the goalpost of lust. With these things pushing me toward the "goalpost," I struggled with lust throughout my teen years. I prayed, cried, punished myself, memorized Scripture and afterward ran right into the goalpost again. I felt like Satan was delighted with me as the pawn in his own version of "Smack Down!"

"smack down!"

can you identify with constant defeat in the face of lust?

Can you identify with constant defeat in the face of lust? Do you sometimes think you're the scum of the earth standing in front of the God of the universe? Have you tried and failed? Congratulations. You qualify! God stands ready to walk with you.

There is hope. I have finally found some of the useable answers that I've been searching for—answers I wished I'd had when I was your age, but all I seemed to hear were tired cliches and slogans like "Let go and let God!" Forget those stupid pep talks. Don't wait for a blinding light. Winning the game of sexual integrity requires a game plan—a set of strategies you live by each day.

If you're ready, let's **rock!**

The bottom line is that we both want to win the game of sexual integrity, right? We need the winningest coach to win such a tough contest. There's only one Coach powerful enough, according to Titus 2:12–13.

Those verses say that God, in His grace, "teaches us to say "No" to worldly passions." Those verses don't offer a simple victory. If you just rest in the fact that you're on "God's team," you'll be blindsided by lust. You have to be willing to be taught, trained, developed, changed, and strengthened. Like a winning athlete, you have to train. You've got to get before the Coach and say, "OK, I know the competition plays dirty and rough, so I need you.

I know the only way I'll win is if you teach me how."

I can't say the game will end. Or that your opponent will never score. The goalpost is always there; and the crowd is always trying to smash your body against it. But one thing I can say: You'll be a contender for sexual integrity if you train under God's grace, fully admitting that only He is qualified to train you for such a contest.

He's not going to do it for you

He's not going to just do it for you. It takes time, discipline, pain, and sweat. You will toil and ache. You will feel yourself stretched beyond your comfort zone. Just when you think that you're ready to play and win, your Coach will call for you to stretch some more.

Are you ready to toil for a victory that won't come easily?

Tell the Coach.

Sexual Integrity Challenge

Sexual Integrity Challenge

You could read what I write all day and never really make any of this stuff work in your life. To make it work, you must do some writing of your own. It's called journaling, guys. It's not so popular these days, but take any great man of the past and you will find pages that recount his extraordinary life. George Washington. Abraham Lincoln. C. S. Lewis. King David. A real journal lets you record what you're doing and feeling and thinking about in response to God's leading your life.

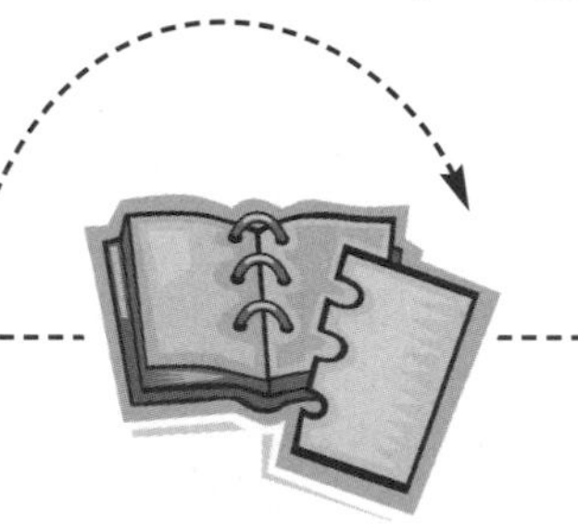

My Story

I'm not a pastor, a counselor, or an expert in the field of sex. I'm just a man. As you will soon see, like every man in the universe, I have struggled to submit to God's plan for sex. Still do. I'm not the poster boy for sexual integrity. (I'm, in fact, a bit afraid of what poster I'd be slapped onto.) There is not one bit of humility, only fear, in me when I say that I don't feel one bit worthy of writing this book. But as I have traveled with my wife, Dannah, who speaks about sexual purity, many young guys have lined up behind me in search of answers. I believe God has asked me to share the secrets I've discovered in battling sexual temptation. For many years I've kept a journal, as I am asking you to do. I've used it to unlock my memory and to remember those moments of failure and success in my own sex life. Nothing I share is made up, but has been retrieved from my journal.

So, dive in with me.

Journaling is, I believe, one of the signs of greatness. Or perhaps, it's just that the time it takes to consider things creates greatness in a man's life.

Now, the thought of keeping a journal may seem intimidating or even nerd-like. As I said, I've learned to endure and even enjoy it sometimes, but I started out feeling very unmotivated, until I found out what it could do in my life. It can revolutionize *your* relationship with God. God blesses—supernaturally intervenes—in the lives of those who embrace His whispers, to those who hear the promptings of the Holy Spirit, and who find direction and comfort in Him. Journaling can help you hear and respond to His voice in a powerful new way. It will also show you where you started and how far you've come.

At the end of each chapter, I will issue a "Sexual Integrity Challenge." In most cases, this can be done in your journal, which can just be a simple spiral-bound notebook. You really need to stop and take this step if you are serious about not getting stomped by lust anymore.

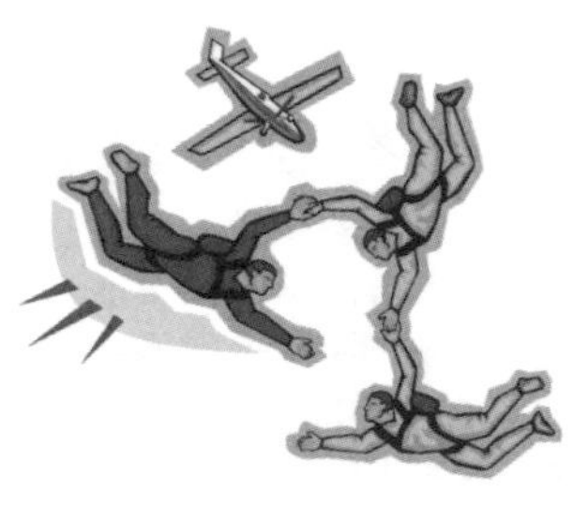

My Friends' Stories

Throughout this book are stories of friends who've influenced my quest for sexual integrity. When you see their first and last names, there has been no alteration to their identity or to the story in any way. In some cases, I will use just a first name, which is fictitious, to honor and protect them. In those cases, I may alter the story just enough to protect that specific person, but be assured the story is real.

Right now I want to challenge you to write a letter to God. You see, knowing Him—really knowing Him—is what will give you a sense of reality. Knowing Him is what will give you the freedom to live uninhibited by the crowd. Stop and ask Him to help you step out of the crowd. Ask Him to speak to you in the silence like never before. And sit in the stillness of that silence to hear His voice.

ask Him to speak to you in the silence like never before

NOTE

1. Rick Reilly, "The NBA Player Who Never Scored" *Sports Illustrated*, December 7, 1999, 100.

Part 1: Satan's Three Sex Lies

CHAPTER 2

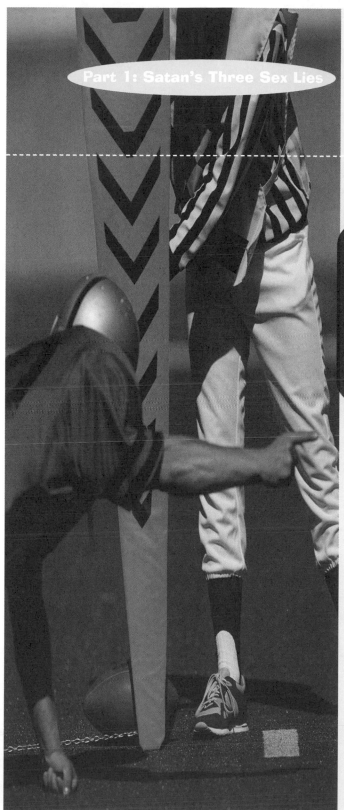

learning to recognize the Truth

> **The devil . . . was a murderer** from the beginning, not holding to the truth, for there is no truth in him. When he lies, he speaks his native language, for he is a liar and the father of lies.
>
> JOHN 8:44

learning to recognize the Truth

The attic was steamy and thick with heat. I could see dust particles dancing in the sun's rays. I smelled old papers and mothballs.

My twelve-year-old mind reeled with confusion.

I'd stumbled onto a magazine. It took only a passing glance of the cover to entice me to look within. A desire was awakened within me that I'd never known as I looked at her. She was beautiful. Every curve said "Yes, look!" So why did I feel something deep within me screaming "No?" I opened it anyway.

I could never have imagined anything that looked so good could make me feel so bad. I started to go throw it away, but sat there wrestling with whether to look again.

I did.

X-X-X-X-O-O-O-O

A naked woman can look absolutely beautiful. God created women to be visually pleasing beyond our wildest dreams. And He created us to crave that beauty. But He's placed some guidelines on our glancing. We get to look all we want . . . at one woman . . . all our lives . . . after we're married. In that setting, the experience is rich and free and fantastic.

Sadly, the beauty of that is being deeply scarred by Satan's sex lies. You see, he is a liar and he loves to lie to us about sex. Jesus tells us the true character of Satan. The devil is "a murderer" and "there is no truth in him."

Every time he opens his mouth, "he lies . . . for he is a liar and the father of lies." Satan persecutes us with his lies.

Sexual temptation is a powerfully deceptive persecution. We expect persecution to involve ridicule, embarrassment, and physical harm. Some of our fellow Christians in other countries risk their lives every day to live for Christ. Some risk their lives just to worship with other believers. That kind of persecution is meant to make a Christian feel so isolated and alone that he shrinks in fear and abandons the faith. Ironically, that kind of open persecution also creates empathy, camaraderie, and resistance. The Christians who face it band together to stand for Christ at any cost.

You and I face a much more subtle persecution . . . sexual temptation. I can worship freely. I can verbally oppose those who believe differently. But everywhere I turn I see nearly naked women . . . hanging on posters in the mall and lined up on magazine racks at convenience stores. I can see the same thing on cable television when I channel surf. I might run into it on the Internet. Think of what sexual temptation does silently, secretly. Giving in to lust creates silent isolation and shame. That's exactly what Satan wants. Why beat it out of us when he can get us to take ourselves out of the competition on our own? What's so ridiculous about the sexual stuff we see is that they're all part of one fantastically designed lie. The women on magazine covers and on mall posters are airbrushed to the max. There's hardly a thread of reality to the images that tempt us. And not many women look like the gorgeous "stars" on TV.

Why beat it out of us when he can get us to take ourselves out of the competition on our own?

that's exactly what Satan wants

I remember once Troy . . . you remember the shoe guy? Anyway, Troy and I were on the beach in South Carolina. I challenged him to find one woman on that stretch of beach who was more beautiful than our wives. He rose to the challenge with me and we walked that beach from one end to the other. Guess what? We were right. Not one of those women came close to Dannah or his wife, Donna. *Not one!* Not *one* woman on that beach looked like *every* woman on TV.

In fact, even the stars on TV don't look like themselves. Have you ever seen pictures of celebrities without their makeup? Hose them down, and most of them are very normal looking and don't match up to their own TV persona.

The December 1990 issue of *Esquire* magazine showed actress Michelle Pfeiffer looking characteristically flawless. *Harper's Magazine* eventually published the bill that *Esquire* got for touching up her photo to get that flawless look.[1] Here's what it looked like:

Esquire/T.Koppel — Invoice

DATE: 11 October 1990
CLIENT: Esquire/T.Koppel
PRODUCT: December Cover/Michelle Pfeiffer

QTY	DESCRIPTION
1	For **Michelle Pfieffer's Beauty**
	DESCRIPTION: Retouching 1 dye transfer two-piece strip of Michelle Pfeiffer in red dress. Clean up complexion, soften eye lines, soften smile line, add color to lips, trim chin, remove neck lines, soften line under ear lobe, add highlights to earrings, add blush to cheek, clean up neck line, remove stray hair, remove hair stands on dress, adjust color and add hair on top of head, add dress on side to create better line, add dress on shoulder, clean up and smooth dress folds under arm and create one seam image on right side.
	TOTAL: $1,525

Source: Duffy Robbins, Harper's, December 1990

I'm *not* saying we can't enjoy the simple beauty of a gorgeous girl. I am saying we have to be careful about craving those glances again and again and again as we imagine her as "ours." That's where lust begins . . . not necessarily in an adult book store. It scares me that I don't have to be in an

adult bookstore to be vulnerable to lust. Even when I'm just walking down the street minding my own business, I find myself so enticed by what I see that I am certain my wife would beat me senseless if she knew what I was thinking! I have been persecuted by illusions . . . lies!

I am certain my wife would beat me senseless if she knew what I was thinking!

Satan's sex lies look a lot like the lies he told Adam and Eve about the Tree of Knowledge of Good and Evil. God's Word tells us that everything in the Garden of Eden was created by God's own hand. It also tells us that He is incapable of making anything that is not good. So, it is very possible that the Tree of Knowledge of Good and Evil would have had quite an interesting and noble purpose. If Adam and Eve had simply waited for God to reveal His purpose to them in His time, who

The Halloween Hoax

Carlisle Indian School vs. Harvard College
October 31, 1903

Glen "Pop" Warner, the legendary 319-win coach was known for his trickery. He once pulled off a Halloween hoax that cost Harvard a touchdown. After one of Warner's players, Jimmie Johnson, settled under a kickoff, his ten teammates huddled around him. Johnson took that opportunity to slip the ball into the jersey of teammate Charlie Dillon, where a rubber band had been sewn in to hold the ball in place. The rest of the Carlisle players removed their brown leather helmets and hugged them close to their chests, creating the illusion that they all had the prized ball. When they scattered, Harvard didn't know who really had the ball. Dillon casually jaunted down the field to score.[2] Boy, does Satan fool us like that. He makes us think that everything coming at us is carrying some promise of pleasure, contentment and fulfillment. We don't know what to tackle and we often end up investing our energy in a futile effort. Sometimes that effort can be costly.

knows what would have happened? Interesting thought, don't you think?

Sex is like that. It is such a good and wonderful thing, and God has created it for a special purpose. We must wait for God's timing to enjoy it. Satan knows that one of the most fabulous things in our world is the sexual union between a husband and a wife when they wait to enjoy it after their wedding day. He wants to rob you of that, so he lies to you.

wait for God's timing

He told my Christian friend Chad that it was OK to experiment sexually. He never had actual intercourse, but Chad did everything else. Recently, he was in his hometown church requesting financial support for his ministry. As he looked across the audience, his eyes fell upon women whom he had defrauded. He was filled with regret.

When I was twelve, Satan told me that "just looking" was OK. I found out the hard way how very much "just looking" can rob you of not just the joy of real sex, but of being a whole and vibrant person.

One of Satan's favorite lies is "everyone is doing it." But studies say that half of your friends were or will be virgins when they graduate from high school. You'd never guess that from watching TV.

Lots of guys help the devil spread his lies. They talk like they are the studs of the universe. How pathetic and spineless when it is not true . . . and it usually isn't. Basketball star A. C. Green, for example, admits he lied about being sexually active in high school.

"I was the biggest liar there was," he admits. "I told everybody whom I did it with, when, how many times. All lies. I mean, don't get me wrong, I wanted to, I just never did. I think, looking back on it, God was protecting me."[3] Today, A.C.'s honesty encourages guys to have the guts to be truthful and to remain virgins until marriage.

Here's another big lie of Satan's. I think he decided there weren't enough guys

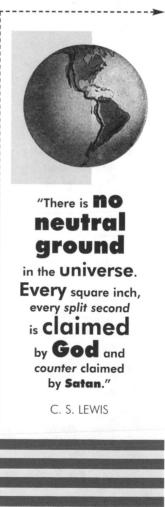

"There is **no neutral ground** in the **universe**. **Every** square inch, every *split second* is **claimed** by **God** and *counter* claimed by **Satan**."

C. S. LEWIS

and women sacrificing their innocence, so he came up with a grand scheme. He got parents and educators to think, "If everyone is doing it and there's something awful like AIDS out there, I had better give my kids tools to do it safely." Now he has educators and sometimes parents saying, "Have safe sex!" Satan's lie is that to keep you safe, we have to teach "safer sex!" The truth is that even *most teenagers* are saying *they* do not want to hear that message. *They* don't believe it's really that safe. In one survey of teens in *USA Today*, 66 percent reported that *they* didn't believe that "safer sex" is safe, but they did believe that it *actually endorses* casual sex. They said they wanted useable skills to enable them to wait.[4]

I don't think that the fear of disease scares many of you enough to keep your zipper up since the passion of the moment seems to win every time, but you should know the facts. So called "safer sex" is one of the most dangerous activities that exists. Condoms, the armor of the "safer-sex" mentality, provide little protection against many sexually transmitted diseases. Although condoms may help, they are not a fail-proof barrier against HIV, the AIDS virus.[5] Condoms provide no protection against herpes or the most common sexually transmitted disease, the human pappilomavirus, which causes more than 2.5 million infections each year. HPV is incurable, uncomfortable, and gross—it causes genital warts in both girls and guys. It causes 90 percent of all cervical cancer in young women and is being linked to other cancers that affect men.[6]

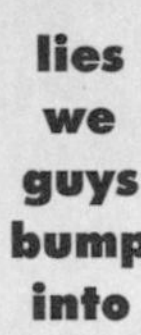

Know this! All of that sickness is a result of misusing God's great gift of sex. Satan is threatened by the existence of such a powerful gift, and he will do anything to see that you do not receive it in the way God has planned.

Of course, Satan uses many lies, and he changes them each time to be just right for each of us. But I see a few common lies that we guys are quite likely to bump into. Pay attention so you can see them coming when he throws them your way. Just take a look at the first big lie in the next chapter. I don't know a guy who hasn't fallen for it.

Sexual Integrity Challenge

What do you think? What lies have you fallen for? Wait! Before you think that you have not been deceived, think about it for a moment. Ask God to reveal anything you might not have seen before. Pray that God will reveal what part of your heart needs to be challenged. This is important. Take the time to write it out to God in your journal or to take a walk while you pray.

NOTES:

1. Duffy Robbins, "It's How You Play the Game," *Harper's*, December 1990, as cited in Mark DeVries, *True Love Waits* (Nashville: Broadman & Holman, 1997), n. p.
2. Brad Herzog, "Whatever It Takes," *US Airways Attaché*, October 2000, 61.
3. Rick Reilly, "The NBA Player Who Never Scored" *Sports Illustrated*, December 7, 1999, 100.
4. Kristine Napier, *The Power of Abstinence* (New York: Avon, 1996), 73.
5. Joshua Mann, Joe S. McIlhaney, Jr., and Curtis C. Stine, "Building Healthy Futures" a report by the Medical Institute of Austin, 2000, 10. Copies are available from the Institute at 800-892-9484.
6. House of Representatives, Rep. Tom Coburn of Oklahoma; "Sexual Health Today: Exploring the Past, Preserving the Future Through Choices Today," a slide presentation provided by the Medical Institute of Austin, Texas. *Congressional Record*, 17 September 1998, H8022.

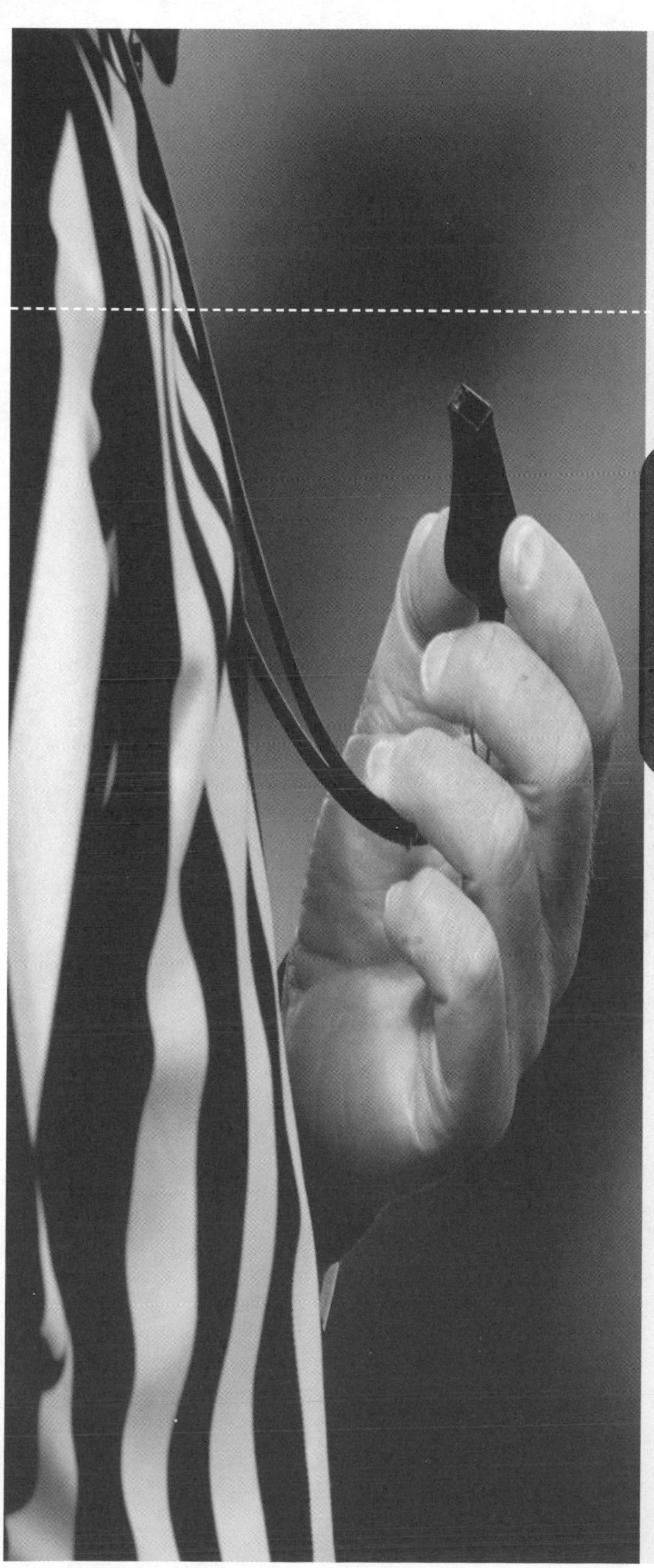

CHAPTER 3

Sex Lie #1

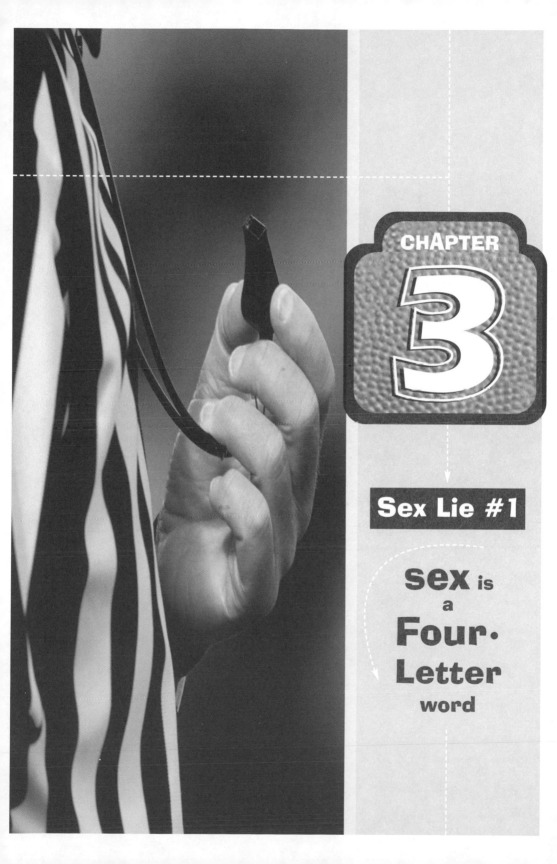

Sex is a Four-Letter word

Now the snake was the best liar of all the animals that God had made. He said to Eve, "Hey, did I hear God say, 'You can't eat from the trees in the garden'?" Eve answered, "Oh, we can eat from the trees in the garden, but God did say 'You must not eat from that tree in the middle of the garden. In fact, don't even touch it or you will die.' "Oh, you won't die," lied the snake. "Come on, God knows that when you bite into that fruit you'll be so full of knowledge. Why, you'll be just like God, knowing good from evil." So Eve looked at the tree and noticed that it was full of fruit and beautiful. Suddenly she believed it would give her wisdom. So she took some and ate it. She also gave some to Adam, who was standing right beside her, and he ate it.

GENESIS 3:1 6 (author paraphrase)

Sex Lie #1

Sex is a Four-Letter word

I'd been struggling for six years now. Last night, I'd gone to church, hoping to find some real answers. Instead, there it was . . . the annual dreaded "flee-youthful-lusts" speech. Anger built inside of me. I remembered thinking, *All I need is a "Honk, If You Love Jesus" bumper sticker and I can head straight to heaven!*

I sat there through the whole thing. My discouragement and shame overwhelmed me. *Why can't I get beyond this sin?* I wondered.

In some moment of sanity, or perhaps insanity, I'd gotten the nerve to approach Pastor Jack. So now I sat in his office, waiting for him to come in.

My sweaty palms clung to the slick wooden chair arms. I shifted back and forth uneasily.

"Hey, Bob," smiled Pastor Jack. He engaged in small talk while my mind wandered off in a self-tormenting battle.

You can back out now, I said to myself. *Don't say anything. Don't do it.*

Do it, I said to myself.

I beat around the bush for maybe a half hour, hoping he'd read my mind. He didn't.

"I'm struggling deeply," I stuttered. "It's . . . well . . . it's all fantasy, I guess, but . . ."

I stalled, hoping he would complete my thoughts. I didn't want to say the *M* word. He just kept listening and letting me go on and on.

When he finally understood, he smiled gently with a look that said, "Oh, is *that* all it is? What an innocent overreaction!"

I felt like a six-year-old kid. I didn't hear what he said in the next few minutes. I was too confused by his reaction. He acted like it was no big deal. He said I was putting too much pressure on myself.

To me it was huge.

I was screaming for help. I wanted someone to take me on as his project. Show me *how* to live out the command I had consistently disobeyed.

All I got was one meeting.

One prayer . . . and a pat on the back.

S-E-X! It's only got three letters. But the way the church treated it when I was a teen made me feel like it was a four-letter word.

Have you seen Steve Irwin, the Croc Hunter on TV? That guy is nuts, but his experience in the swamps reminds me of a story told by Tommy Nelson, a pastor in Texas. It sums up how I was feeling during this period in my life.

Once upon a time there was a man who visited a community of people who lived by a river. As evening approached, he was invited to sit down by the river and enjoy a cool beverage and then dinner with the people. While they ate calmly and pleasantly, a fourteen-foot crocodile suddenly came up out of the river, chomped off the arm of the man sitting closest to the riverbank and then slipped silently back

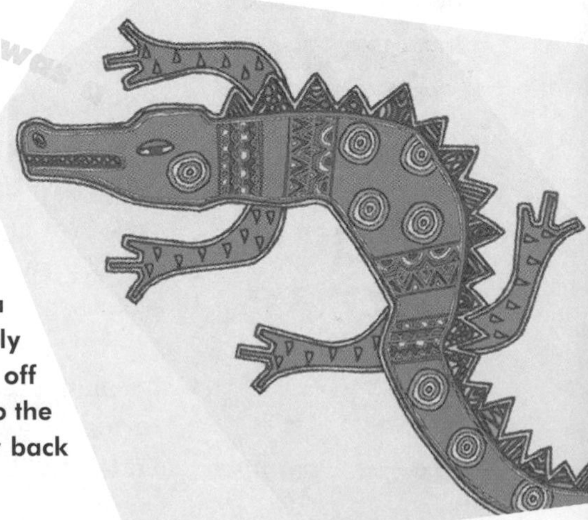

into the dark waters. The people were alarmed and shocked, but they recomposed themselves. Those closest to the man bandaged him up the best they could and transported him to medical assistance. Then they resumed their eating, drinking and conversation—picking up right where they left off without any discussion of the incident.

The visiting man was horrified that the evening continued as if nothing had happened. Each time he tried to mention the tragic and violent act, someone in the group quickly changed the subject. He made one final attempt to bring up the incident to discuss: "A man just lost his arm to an enormous crocodile that came suddenly out of the river. Didn't you all see that, or was I imagining things?"

Someone in the group replied, "Yes, I saw what happened. A number of people are attacked each year in our community by crocodiles."

The man then looked closer at the group and sure enough, he spotted people who were missing hands and feet, fingers and ears. "Can't you do anything about the crocodiles?" he asked.

Another in the group replied with embarrassment clearly written on his face, "It is impolite in our culture to talk about crocodiles."

The visitor to the community was stunned into bewildered silence.[1]

I really feel like that's how the church deals with sex. We just pretend it's not there. While growing up in church, I never heard the word *masturbation.* I'm not sure I heard it at my Christian college either. Every guy is thinking about it and has questions, but who's talking about it? I bet you can look around your church and see friends and families who have been deeply affected by sexual sin, but who's helping them through the hurt? Who's giving Christians useable tools to live a life of sexual integrity? Who's giving them advice on how to bind those great big scars with God's healing and forgiveness?

The world screams a message that makes sex seem common, casual, and cheap, but we don't find the church talking about it much. Author Ed Young writes:

> **Based on what is depicted by the media, any alien visitor to America would likely conclude that every person over the age of twelve is sexually active, that marriage is the last place to look for sexual satisfaction, that faithfulness is a nostalgic dream, and that even the sickest of perversions is nothing less than every citizen's "inalienable right."**
>
> **This would be true, of course, unless they happened to visit the church. Then they would probably wonder whatever became of sex. They might never hear it mentioned at all—or perhaps only spoken of in whispers or condemning tones. Historically, to its shame, the church has either ignored the God-given gift of human sexuality or smothered it in an avalanche of "Thou-shalt-nots."[2]**

As a teen, my church's annual "thou-shalt-not" speech, didn't give me useable tools to live a life of sexual integrity. It probably wasn't intentional, but that speech did a great job of making me feel like dirt. The secrecy made me feel like sex was a dirty word and that my curiosity made my "dark side" one big dirty secret.

Pastor Bill Perkins concludes that "unfortunately many churches actually create an environment in which sexual addictions thrive. Why? Because secrecy and risk increase the adrenaline rush associated with sexual sins. In a sense, they act like a turbocharger that infuses a man's lust with a powerful surge of energy."[3]

do not think about the polar bear

Secrecy creates uncontrollable curiosity. In one study of college students, an instructor showed the class a picture of a big white polar bear at the beginning of his lecture. With some of his classes, he put the bear away and then said, "Whenever you think of this polar bear, please push the button at your desk." A few thought about that bear during the class, but not many. With some of his classes, he put the polar bear picture away and then said, "It is very important that you *do not* think about this polar bear during this class. *Do not* think about it, but if you do, please push the button at your desk." The classes that were told not to think about it overwhelmingly thought about it repeatedly throughout the entire class.[4] A lot like sex, huh?

Sex... A Blessed Gift

Sex is *not* a four-letter word. Sex is an absolutely amazing gift which God is proud to give to us

God loves sex. Just look at Solomon's sexually graphic "song" about his honeymoon. Just before he puts down his pen, he lets us hear the last words uttered on that sensual night when God Himself comes to bless their night of ecstasy. The Lord Himself said, "Eat, O friends, and drink; drink your fill, O lovers."[5] God honors sexuality.

God knew what He was doing when He created women to be utterly tempting. He masterfully sculpted their eyes, lips, hair, legs, breasts, hips, and legs . . . oh, I already said "legs!" He made them to be just what Adam needed to fill the void of loneliness—a void that God couldn't meet in any other way, even by His own presence. (Imagine that!)

A woman's body is a carefully crafted masterpiece. Sex is the gift God gives us to receive that masterpiece as a part of us. There's no big secret about it—just simple, fantastic, beautiful truth.

God wants us to wait and there's a good reason for that. One study by Tim and Beverly LaHaye found that married couples who had not engaged in premarital intercourse were more likely to be sexually satisfied.[6] An extensive study completed by a University of Chicago research team found that those who report the greatest sexual satisfaction are the married couples.[7]

God's Word promises that very thing in Deuteronomy 6:24 when it says,

The Secret Player

Georgia vs. Alabama
October 26, 1912

A lone water boy once came to the rescue in a creative 1912–13 University of Georgia football game. The guy scored in their October game against the University of Alabama. If a spectator had taken time to count, it would have appeared that Georgia was playing with only ten men. But there was an eleventh. A player named Alonzo Autrey was standing on the sidelines dressed in coveralls and holding a bucket of water. Alabama, of course, ignored the water boy, but just as Georgia snapped the ball, Autrey dumped the bucket to race down the field to catch a 30-yard pass. The deceitful play caused a riot in the stands that had to be broken up by police, but the play stood and Georgia won 13–9. Never assume you know the truth of a situation. Deceit isn't easy to identify. On the contrary, you might think you're playing on a clean field with a friendly water boy nearby when in truth your opponent is planning to sock it to you.

"The Lord commanded us to obey all these decrees . . . so that we might always *prosper*!" The writer was talking about all the laws God had just given. Their purpose, he explained, was to make the nation of Israel prosperous. I see that trend throughout Scripture. God desired for Israel then—and He desires for you and me today—to live strong, healthy, vibrant prosperous lives. He doesn't ask us to wait to have sex just to frustrate us (though it may do just that!). He knows how much more fulfilling sex will be if we wait.

did I hear God say . . . ?

Stand firm! Ephesians 5:3 says that within the church, "there must not be even a hint of sexual immorality, or of any kind of impurity."

News flash! Knowing that God wants us to wait doesn't help us avoid the problem of lust. In the Garden, Adam and Eve knew what God wanted. He wanted them to wait. Satan used the very commandment of God to tempt them. He asked, "Did I hear God say . . . ?"

Satan tempted Adam and Eve to sin[9] just like he tempts you and me today. In the first temptation, the snake slithered up to them and tried to get the inside track by talking about some classified information. "Hey, did I hear God say you can't eat from any trees in the garden?" Of course, he twisted God's Word to include all the trees, not just the Tree of the Knowledge of Good and Evil. Sounds like his lies today about sex—making us feel like we are missing it all, forever, completely.

It reminds me of the way the church treats sex. In our secrecy, we help Satan stretch the truth to make us feel like abstinence is about simply not having sex . . . about missing the party. I don't even like the word *abstinence,* because it suggests a negative position. Sexual integrity is all about pursuing purity. It's a positive choice!

stand firm! it's a positive choice!

I think the reason sex is treated like such a dirty word in the church is because there is far more than a hint of sexual immorality in us. We are ashamed and so, like Adam and Eve in the Garden, we hide. We hide from the truth of our sin, and in doing so, we take with it the truth of God's gift. Since the church stays silent, we hear only the stupid, twisted sexual messages of the world. And our ears are all too willing to listen. That's a powerful reason for the church to step out from behind its wall of secrecy and talk about sex like God does—with respect and honor.

Get ready. It's time to talk serious sex.

No secrets.

No shame.

Sexual Integrity Challenge

On a blank page in your journal, I want you to write down every single shameful secret you can think of. That doesn't sound comfortable, does it? But, don't worry. No one will see this list. After you write it, I want you to pray that God would rip these lies right out of your mind. Then, rip that page out of your journal and into a thousand pieces. No, that won't fix it all, but it's an invigorating beginning.

NOTES

1. Tommy Nelson, *The Book of Romance* (Nashville: Thomas Nelson, 1998), 86.
2. Ed Young, *Pure Sex* (Sisters, Ore.: Multnomah, 1997), 18.
3. Bill Perkins, *When Good Men Are Tempted* (Grand Rapids: Zondervan: 1997) , 38.
4. "Suppress Now, Obsess Later," *Journal of Personality and Social Psychology*, vol. 53.
5. Song of Songs 5:1. The sexually graphic references appear throughout Solomon's Song, both in poetic references to pomegranates and apples (which were not actually apples, but pomegranates) that depict juicy, ripe, seed-filled fruit that harken to the fruitfulness of the human body and the sexual organs (for example, 2:5; 4:13), and sensual references to the human body (for example, 5:10–16; 6:1–10).
6. Tim and Beverly LaHaye, *The Act of Marriage* (Grand Rapids: Zondervan, 1976), 210.
7. Robert T. Michael, John H. Gagnon, Edward O. Laumann, and Gina Kolata, *Sex in America* (New York, Warner Books:1994), 124.
8. Ephesians 5:3; 1 Corinthians 6:12,18 (NLT)
9. See Genesis 3:1–6.

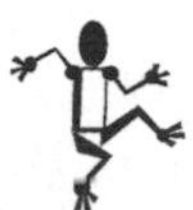

Sex Lie #2

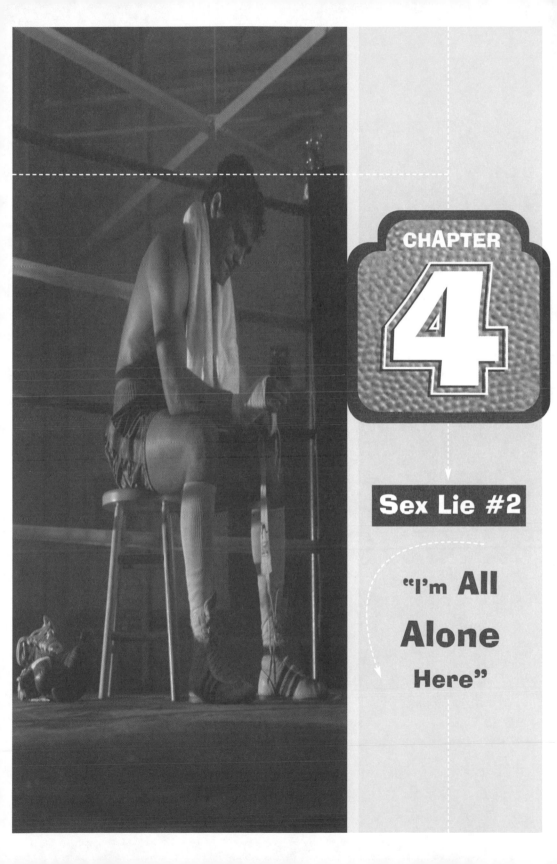

“I’m All Alone Here”

> **Don't waste your time on** . . .
> the barren pursuits of darkness. Expose these things for the sham they are. It's a scandal when people waste their lives on things they must do in the darkness where no one will see. Rip the cover off those frauds and see how attractive they look in the light of Christ.
>
> EPHESIANS 5:12–14 *(The Message)*

CHAPTER 4

Sex Lie #2

"I'm All Alone Here"

My roommate Jamie could tease a guy into total aggravation. He'd been doing a lot of that lately.

Last weekend Troy and I had spent the afternoon on the deck grabbing some springtime sunshine. Jamie had come to join us. Every few minutes a splatter of raindrops would fall across us. We'd grumble and look around, but the sky looked clear. Where was that water coming from? This went on for an hour or two when suddenly one of us noticed a water gun by Jamie's side.

"You dirty dog," I said. "Knock that off!"

"What?" Jamie asked as if he was completely puzzled.

"Quit it," grumbled Troy.

After a few minutes, another splatter of "rain." This time we caught Jamie on the draw and exposed his battery-operated water pistol. Chaos ensued.

That was all fun, but the following days brought more splatters of "rain." On the deck, in the kitchen, in the living room, in our bedrooms. Everywhere we went, Jamie's rainfall seemed to follow. It was never a good, robust squirt, just an annoying, irritating drop. Consistent. Juvenile. Torturous.

Today was payback. Operation Downpour was about to begin.

> today was payback

Troy's girlfriend, Donna, was at the top of the second-deck steps. Cool cat that she was, she sat in a lawn chair with her feet up on a paint bucket, pretending to catch some rays. She was bucket number one.

Troy was in my bedroom, which was also on the second floor but right above the middle of the outer stairs. The window was open and the screen was out. Troy was poised with bucket number two.

I had the high-stress mission of waiting for Jamie and then casually jumping out of my car which I'd "just arrived in," grabbing bucket number three, which just happened to be at the base of the stairs. I had to be there just as Jamie was halfway up the stairs and directly under the window.

The sound of wheels on gravel . . . time for

Operation Downpour! to begin.

I didn't look up.

One door slammed. Another door slammed.

Feet on gravel.

"Hey, geekster," greeted Jamie as he passed me. A large pizza box was in his hands. This was going to be sweeter than I had thought.

this was going to be sweeter than I thought

I stood up and shut the door to my car. Jamie was heading up the stairs. I approached water bucket number three. I reached for it.

"Hey, Jamie!" I called. He was almost halfway up the stairs. "We collected all those drops of 'rain' we've been having around here."

I held up my bucket. He looked at me as if to say, "Catch me if you can!"

"There was one problem," I continued. "They wouldn't fit in one bucket."

A new look came over Jamie's face.

He looked up at Donna, who now stood carefully poised with bucket number one and a valiant smirk on her face.

"Hey, Jamie," taunted Troy from above.

I remember it as if it were in slow motion.

It was better than slow motion. As Jamie looked up, Troy's water came down. Donna and I sprung into action.

As if in some perfect dance of satisfaction, the three arcs of water converged perfectly together covering their target from head to toe.

my worst nightmare

"Operation Downpour complete," I announced as the laughter echoed down the alley.

Jamie and Troy were like brothers. The three of us were together day and night, so I was never alone. But I was always lonely. In the middle of all that fun and laughter, I actually felt utterly and completely alone.

It had been just a few weeks since Jamie and Troy had lovingly but awkwardly confronted me with their suspicions. They could tell that I was struggling with lust. I'm not sure they really knew the extent of it, but their loving confrontation was my worst nightmare. I was busted. Neither of them seemed to struggle with lust . . . or if they did, they sure weren't saying so.

No one had seemed to know what to say. It was a brief conversation made up of stumbling phrases and awkward looks. I kept waiting for it to come up again. I almost had hoped it would in some awful way.

I felt like I was all alone

I felt like I was all alone. And now, even when my friends were near, I was all alone.

←------------X-X-X-X-O-O-O-O---------→

Read this next sentence a few times until you get it:

You are not alone.

If you are struggling with lust or are just plain curious about sex, **you are not alone.** Lust is the universal mark of every man living in the fallen world of sin. A University of Chicago sex study said that 54 percent of men thought about sex daily—a number that caused humorist Dave Barry to conclude, "The other 46 percent of the men are lying. Because it's a known scientific fact that all men think about sex a minimum of all the time." [1]

Get ready; we are going deep for a minute. I'm going to present some statistics to prove that **you are not alone.** I fear that some of you might try to use these facts to justify a sinful habit. But I think the risk is worth it for the courage that you can gain through this.

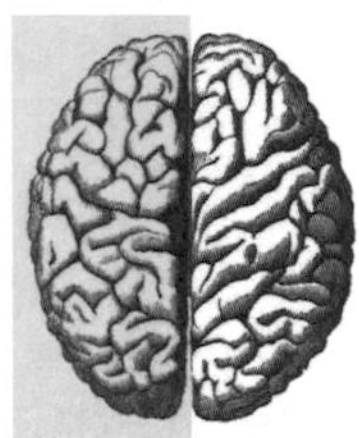

Is Masturbation a Sin?

It would be nice if the Bible answered that question, but it doesn't. Instead, we have varied opinions from some of today's most respected leaders. Christian authors Dr. Clifford and Joyce Penner feel that it "relieves the physical need and may be helpful in self-discovery." Authors Tim and Beverly LaHaye are sympathetic with those views but "feel it is an unacceptable practice for Christians" for several reasons.[2] I tend to lean toward the LaHayes' opinion because the Bible clearly says that fantasizing and lustful thoughts are wrong.[3] If you are fantasizing about a girl or looking at pornography while you masturbate, it is clearly sin. Let's face it, fantasy and masturbation are virtually inseparable. Another reason Christians need to avoid masturbation is because it can become habit forming and inflame a guy's desire to fantasize. This desire can continue long after he is married,

(continued on page 43)

Are You Struggling with "the M Word"?

OK, here's the most taboo word in the Christian lexicon: *masturbation*. You might as well get used to the word because you're going to deal with it a lot, and it's no worse a word than any other.

At a retreat recently, I mentioned masturbation, and it struck fear into the guys. I went on to say, "Hey, they've finally come up with an actual test to determine whether a guy has masturbated or not. Although the test isn't perfect, what we do is this. We take a guy into a room. We strip off his pants, then we strip off his underwear. If he has a penis, he's masturbated." The group sat in stunned silence for a second as they processed the joke, but then a roar of laughter broke out. The wall of secrecy and shame that every guy was hiding behind started to crumble and fall.

the masturbation test

Masturbation is a common issue for guys. A survey of college men found that 88 percent of them had masturbated at least once.[3]

The rest? The joke I keep hearing is that the other 12 percent are lying.

If you have struggled with or are struggling with masturbation,

you are not alone.

Are You Struggling with Pornography?

Most men struggle with pornography. Magazines, videos, and the Internet take out nearly all of us at one time or another. In fact, *sex* is the most frequently used search word on the Internet. And many experts credit Pamela Lee Anderson with the rapid growth of the Internet. (Come on! You thought she was popular for her acting??!!)

A survey at one Promise Keepers conference revealed that 50 percent of the men who attended the event had viewed pornography *during the week leading up to the conference.*[6] I'm not surprised by the percentages. I'm surprised by how well we keep our secret.

If you have struggled with or are struggling with the use of pornography,

you are not alone.

(continued from page 42)

causing him to (1) not minister to his wife's sexual needs and (2) think of or look at other women when he fantasizes. Scripture speaks harshly of both of these practices.[4] The Hebrew word for sin was actually an ancient archery term which basically means "to miss the bullseye." In other words, sin is anything off course of God's intended best for you. God made our sexual desires to be expressed within marriage with our wives. That's His best for your sexual desires. Don't squander it.

Are You Struggling with Sexual Activity with Girls You Date?

A recent study of Christian teens showed that 43 percent had experienced sexual intercourse by age eighteen.[7] That doesn't include those who have engaged in fondling of the breasts or genitals and other sexual exploration.

If you have struggled with or are struggling with the sexual activity with girls you date,

you are not alone.

I better say this one more time. Don't let this information become an excuse for your sin. It is sin. It can have long-term, harmful effects. But know this . . .

you are not alone.

Satan uses our isolation and shame to keep us from dragging our sin into the light. He stops our progress toward living a life of sexual integrity and feeds the monster of lust with loneliness. Soon the sin and the shame can take over our relationships with family and friends and even God. It happened to me. In my clumsy attempts to reach out to Christian leaders, my shame only grew. Some of them, I now believe, were trying to reduce that shame by not making such a big deal out of things, but that only fed my sin. As I felt alone and embarrassed, I'd look to sexual stimulation to ease the pain. Eventually, I felt like the relationship I had with God was blocked by a thick wall of sinful secrets and shame.

If you can come to understand that

you are not alone,

you will have the courage to reach out for help. James 5:16 says to "confess your sins to each other so that you may be healed." Coming out into the light—confessing—is the place of our healing. As someone older and wiser hears your confessions, he can verbalize God's forgiveness. As he encourages you, you will feel God's forgiveness. Make no mistake; only God can forgive, but He gives us each other to help us to let go of things and to keep us accountable.

Today there is a healthier dialogue about the temptation men face than there was when I was in high school. The Promise Keepers men's movement has broken through much of the secrecy. You can find a man who might not have all the answers but will take the time to talk with you about

you are not alone

your frustrations. He will help you let go of sinful habits. That's something you can't do by yourself.

Have you heard about the easiest way to trap a monkey? Place a banana in a jar. The monkey can get his hand into the jar, but when he is clenching the banana, he can't get his hand out. The monkey will want the banana so badly that he won't let go—he won't let go even if men come to cage him.

break through the secrecy

That's so much like sexual temptation. We grab it. We recognize the danger at some level but we just don't let go.

It's time to let go.

It's time to bring it into the light. Tell an older, wiser friend.

Clay Crosse on Being Alone

BOB: A lot of guys are afraid to talk about their struggles with lust because they think they are alone in this—that they are the only one struggling.

CLAY: No. The person would be alone who is not in this! The guy who says I am not tempted by, say Victoria's Secret commercials or just everything in our society, that guy—he's the one that's alone.

BOB: Have you met that guy yet? . . . cause I keep trying to meet this guy. Have you found him?

CLAY: No. I never have.

Satan's lie is that you are alone. You must know that you are not alone so that you'll courageously reach out to Christian men for confession and accountability. I wish I had understood that much sooner, because I've got news for you . . . it never gets any easier. Just take a look at the last big lie you probably believe.

Sexual Integrity Challenge

Now, knowing that you're not alone, it's time to drag everything into the light. Whether you're just beginning to sense the taunting of lust or you're in the midst of full-fledged sexual sin, it's time to reach out.

It may not be easy or comfortable. You may have to work for awhile to find the right guy; but make sure you do it! Prolonging the confession only makes you miserable longer. Trust me when I say if I'd known how freeing it was I wouldn't've gotten accountability much sooner. Who can you talk to? Is there someone older and wiser in your life who you can approach boldly for accountability? Your youth pastor, a young married guy or maybe your dad are some good resources. Why not touch base with one of them right now?

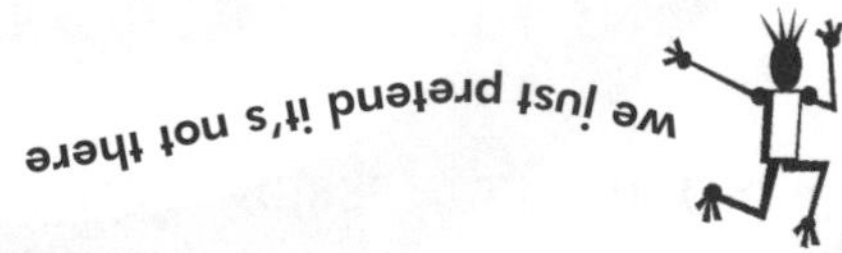
we just pretend it's not there

NOTES

1. As cited in Ed Young, *Pure Sex* (Sisters, Ore.: Multnomah, 1997), 81.
2. Clifford and Joyce Penner, *The Gift of Sex* (Waco, Tex.: Word, 1981), 236; and Tim and Beverly LaHaye, *Raising Sexually Pure Kids* (Sisters, Ore.: Multnomah 1998), 105. To read the position of Dr. James Dobson, president of Focus on the Family, see Appendix B, letter 3.
3. Matthew 5:28.
4. 1 Corinthians 7:3–5; Matthew 5:28.
5. Leland Elliot and Cynthia Brantley, *Sex on Campus* (New York, Random House: 1997), 28.
6. Laurie Hall, *An Affair of the Mind* (Colorado Springs: Focus on the Family, 1996), 236.
7. Josh McDowell and Bob Hostettler, *Right from Wrong* (Dallas, Word: 1994), 27.

CHAPTER 5

Sex Lie #3

"It'll go away When I'm Married"

As he thinks within himself, so he is.

PROVERBS 23:7 (NASB)

Chapter 5

Sex Lie #3

"It'll go away When I'm Married"

The atmosphere last night had been just right. The loud music had pulsed through me, igniting strong passion. The crowd, ironically, created anonymity. I didn't know her that well. She didn't know me that well. I'd never expected her to notice me like this. She looked so good. Her words dripped with invitation. She was willing if I was.

It could have been my finest hour, but I was caught up in the moment and now I was left with the deep loneliness of my shame. I sat alone in my car thinking. Then I reached for my journal and wrote. "My failure last night and today is unbelievable. I have lost all bearings on my life and am drifting further and further without any guidance to lead me back."

I put my pen down. I was seventeen, and from my sports car I could see Junior High West. Memories of a time when life was simpler flooded my soul. Little league, gym class, football—all those things seemed so glorious. With a silly grin, I began to ponder my "extensive" junior high football "career," only to have my mind rushed back into the reality of last night.

Last night hadn't ended so badly in comparison to some stories I'd heard. It hadn't gone beyond reckless, passionate kissing. But hours later my mind had taken it so much further.

I'd given up hope of controlling this sexual hunger before I was married. I longed to fast-forward and know who my wife would be. I wanted to save all of this for her, but it was a frightening reality that I feared not making it.

If only I could.

I was certain that once I was married it would all go away.

In a Promise Keepers newsletter I was reading, a guy described his struggle with sexual temptation. He was introduced to pornography when he was eleven. His fascination grew quickly. During his teen years, he gave his life to Christ and believed it would stop his use of the pornography. It didn't. When he finally got married, he was aware that he was a sex addict. He wrote: "I know it will sound hypocritical, but because of my Christian beliefs, I stayed a virgin until I was married. I assumed when I got married the preoccupation would chill out."

It didn't.

"Our wedding night was a big disappointment. I'd brought the only sexual experience I knew into a loving relationship, and there was no connection. . . . I was crushed with the realization that my wife wasn't exciting."[1]

Shortly after he was married, he was using pornography again.

Almost every guy I've ever talked to believed (or still does believe) this lie. After all, it makes sense. We think, "If sex is available with my wife, why would I need anything else?"

your wedding day will not be the finish line

When Will the Temptation End?

Your wedding day will not be the finish line when it comes to sexual temptation. It wasn't for King David.

God called David "a man after my own heart."[2] He had prayerfully led God's people to many victories. He'd composed some of the most beautiful words of worship man has known. He'd been a faithful shepherd to his people as the ruler of Israel for approximately twenty years. He was not a pervert or a sex addict as some would like to portray. He was a man who loved God.

But he was . . . a man. He too fell for the lie that you and I often believe when we hope that our struggles with sexual temptation will end when we are married. In *David: A Man of Passion and Destiny,* Charles Swindoll concluded:

Even though his wives and concubines increased, his passion was not abated. This king who took another man's wife already had a harem full of women. The simple fact is that the passion of sex is not satisfied by a full harem of women; it is increased. Having many women does not reduce a man's libido, it excites it . . . it stimulates it. David, being a man with a strong sexual appetite, mistakenly thought, *To satisfy it, I will have more women. Thus, when he became the king, he added to the harem, but his drive only increased.* One of the lies of our secular society is that if you just satisfy this drive, then it'll be abated.[3]

I added those bold italics because I don't want you to miss what Pastor Swindoll just said there about society's big lie. And what a lie it is!

David was disobeying God when he was adding wives to his house. God had clearly told him not to do that.[4] To him it was a way to feed his sexual drive and, after all, it was socially acceptable. To God, it was not OK. David believed he could satisfy lust through marriage and concubines. He could not.

It's still happening today. Christian recording artist Michael English ruined his marriage and Christian music career with an adulterous affair. Was he living in a cesspool of sexual sin and wild nightly parties? On the contrary, English was married and singing for God at sold-out concerts. Just days before the affair broke, he walked away with an armload of Dove music awards and the applause of the entire Christian music industry. He was closely connected with Bill Gaither, a man of great Christian integrity. Michael's song, "I want to see Jesus," which he once performed with the Gaither Vocal Band, is one of the few songs that deeply moves my heart. Before news of his affair broke, it looked as if he was at the top of the world. His fall is a reminder to all men: All

it's still happening today

of our service and love for God does not keep us protected from lust.

join the club

He's not alone. Other prominent Christian leaders have fallen flat on their faces because of lust. Godly Christian men fall every day. Married men who have the full right to express themselves sexually with the wife God has given them find themselves still struggling with lust.

Do you believe that your sexual appetite will subside once you can express it within the confines of marriage? Join the club. We all believe it at some point. But it doesn't work like that. You see, lust and fantasizing have almost nothing to do with sex.

I was a virgin on my wedding day. I had never had sex with another woman. But my mind had been sexually active many, many times. My appetite for pushing the limit to feed my lust had been continually pacified. I *wanted* to experience pleasure and believed it would make me feel good about *me*.

Lust is a selfish, chemically driven bondage to sexual substitutes. It's all about how we view ourselves as men—what we think about ourselves.

it's all about how we view ourselves

Let's think about it. If you look at a woman and fantasize about her, it's not real, right? Or is it? Well, something else is going on. When our bodies experience erection and ejaculation as a result of fantasizing about that woman, she becomes real to the brain. Chemicals are again released, one of which is adrenaline. This creates a rush of mood alteration which can be followed by a narcotic-like effect . . . you're high![5] The chemicals give us a false sense of reality. And since the fantasy is, after all, *ours* we tend to be Superman-like sex machines.

Or maybe, like me, you've even had moments where sexual temptation was about more than just curiosity and selfish pleasure-seeking. Sometimes it is about trying to make life better because things are out of control. Through sexual fantasy, we may create this mental view of ourselves because the fantasy makes us feel like we are in control. Maybe we can't control whether we make the team or if dad comes home or not, but in our fantasy world of lust, everything is just as we want it to be.

Clay Crosse On Marriage

Bob: One of the lies that Satan feeds us guys says that if you struggle with this before marriage, it'll go away when you get married.

Clay: I thought that too. I really did. For a few years it *was* different. I didn't want pornography in my life. Eventually it crept back in. It was probably six years into our marriage. For some guys I am sure it's a lot sooner than that. You can't look at marriage as being your savior. Christ is our Savior.

(For Clay's whole story, see page 186–189).

When marriage comes along and everything doesn't happen just like in our fantasies, we find ourselves frustrated and unfulfilled by what should be fantastic and fun. We can't find the satisfaction that God meant for us to know. We've robbed our own marriage bed.

Proverbs 23:7 says that "as [a man] thinks within himself, so he is."[6]

So what are you? What's in the think tank of your heart? What's the reality you have of yourself?

Satan's plan is to bind you not only physically to lust but also to bind your heart. He wants to numb your heart to God's reality. He uses another dimension to do this rather than the world itself. It's a battle that's taking

"Choose your **rut** carefully. You'll be **in it** *for the* *next* **200** miles."

A sign on an Alaska highway

place in your own head. Paul tells us in 2 Corinthians 10:4–5 that we aren't fighting a battle that's real or visible or of this world. Satan introduces something new and binding through lust. Lust is not a battle that takes place between your legs. The struggle with lust is in your head. It's about how you think about yourself.

You might be a virgin physically, but are you a virgin mentally? Are you praying that your sexual appetite will be quenched by your wife's passion one day? If you are feeding lust and believe that it'll be satisfied when you're married, think again. The appetite you're feeding won't go away that easily.

Author Brent Sapp told this story about a visit he and his daughter had in an exotic pet store:

One glass case was filled with very cute lizards—that's right, cute lizards. They were about five inches long and had big, friendly eyes—almost like a Labrador Retriever. Just take my word for it; they were cute.

When the store's owner saw us pausing to look at the lizards, he took one out for us to hold. It snuggled in my hand and almost purred as my daughter and I petted it. "What's the name of this type of lizard?" I asked.

"It's a Savannah Monitor," the owner said.

"Is this as big as it gets?" I asked, still petting the calm lizard.

"Oh, no," he responded. "In fact, there's a grown Savannah over there." We followed him around the corner to a much larger cage encased with thick wire. Inside was a reptile about four feet long that looked like it was on loan from the movie "Lost World." When my daughter and I stepped closer, the big lizard whipped around and snapped at the front of the cage.

"Yep," said the owner. "You can walk one around on a leash when it gets this size, but it'll drag you around a

> **bit. You'd have to close in your backyard, of course." Then he added, "I wouldn't let children walk back there, though."**
>
> **I found it hard to believe that a little, purring reptile I'd help in my hand a few minutes earlier could one day look at my children the way I look at a cheese pizza!**
>
> **Bad habits are a lot like that cute little lizard. At first a bad habit seems harmless, and we don't believe there is any way it could hurt us. We get comfortable with it, feed it and soon it begins to grow. Before long, it consumes more time and effort than before. In fact, the habit can become so strong that it is difficult to control. Soon, it gets so powerful that it can start to control us and drag us around.** [7]

Sapp went on to compare playing with lust and sexual temptation to playing with a baby T-rex. It's a dangerous—though at the time somewhat controllable—thrill. But the thrill will grow bigger and bigger. And it will have an appetite capable of devouring you . . . even after you are married.

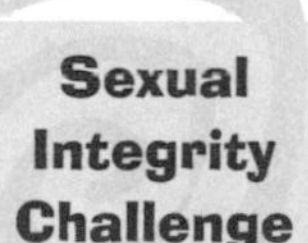

Sexual Integrity Challenge

Are you cuddling up to any lizards that could grow into uncontrollable monsters? Have you believed the lie that those lizards won't be around once you're married? Why not stop right now, get on your knees, and pray once again that God's grace would train you to live a life of sexual integrity?

NOTES

1. "Obsessed and Consumed: Emerging from the Prison of Pornography," *The Promise Keeper* newsletter, July/August 1998, 1.
2. Acts 13:22; 1 Samuel 13:14.
3. Charles R. Swindoll, *David: A Man of Passion and Destiny* (Dallas: Word, 1997), 182.
4. Deuteronomy 17:17.
5. Mark R. Laaser, *Faithful and True: Sexual Integrity in a Fallen World* (Grand Rapids: Zondervan, 1992), 26.
6. New American Standard Bible
7. Brent Sapp, "Teknon and the Champion Warriors: Mission Guide-Son"; a booklet from Family Life ministry of Little Rock, Arkansas, 87–88.

CHAPTER 6

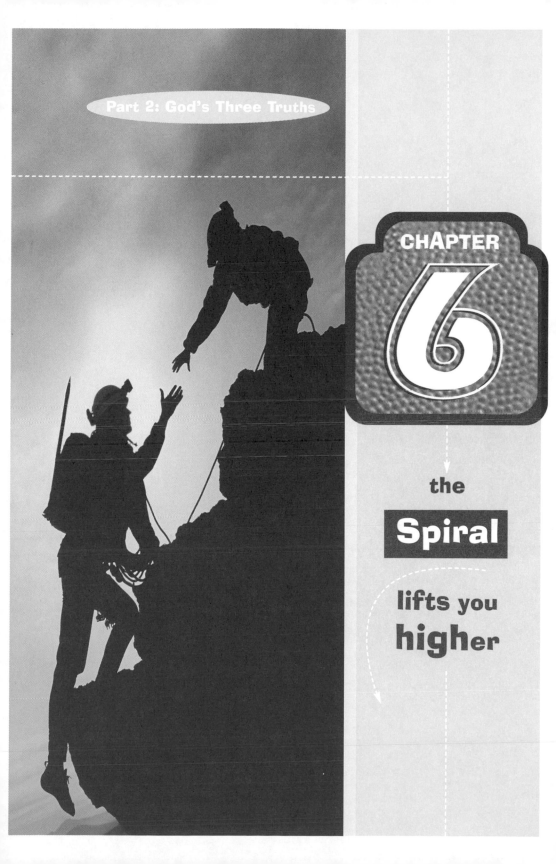

the Spiral lifts you higher

[God desires] that you become blameless and pure.

PHILIPPIANS 2:15

the Spiral lifts you higher

I wanted to shout out loud as I ran up the path to my cabin at World of Life Island. I could have run the entire beach on the island nestled in the middle of Schroon Lake in the Adirondack Mountains.

As I ran along, I thought how pitiful and ashamed I had felt when camp began. I felt like a hypocrite because of my never-ending, ever-losing battle with lust. I sure felt different now.

Camp had been better than great this year.

I'd won my fair share of Fruit of the Loom waistbands from the mighty wedgie matches and beaten the neighboring cabin in the unofficial, camp-banned competition of practical jokes. And I'd just made the most amazing commitment of my life.

Tonight at the campfire as we sang, I knew I'd met my Savior in a new way. I knew He'd miraculously removed the shame and the temptation. It was gone. It had to be. I'd thrown that stick onto the fire and that was that.

I had no idea that for the next six years I would return to camp with that same feeling of hypocrisy, only to run this same pathway after throwing another stick onto the fire.

I'd burn a lot of wood.

Roller coasters! They give a great rush of adrenaline. The Rockin' Roller Coaster at Disney's MGM Studios is one of the best roller coaster rushes

I've ever experienced. They strap you into your "stretch limo" seat in the back of an alley. You watch "road signs" in front of you which signal your departure. I am convinced they have to do that or your body could not handle what comes next. Within 2.8 seconds you move from a stationary position to 60 miles per hour. That first six seconds is an out-of-body experience. Riders experience nearly 5 "Gs" in comparison to the 3 "Gs" experienced by astronauts at liftoff. The rest of the roller coaster ride is in the dark, orchestrated to music. Just as you are about to reach a tumultuous turn, a black light comes on and illuminates a road sign ahead. Again, I think they really have to do that or the ride would be sheer torture. The split-second knowledge of the loop or side flip turns the terror into a rush of squeamish fun.

you know that feeling, don't you?

I used to wish my real-life roller coaster was like that . . . came with some signs of warning. But in general, my spiritual roller coaster always operated in total, fearful darkness, and always took me back to where I started. Do you ever get the feeling that your spiritual life is a roller coaster? One week you are overwhelmed by your pathetic state of sin and the next you are on your way "up and out!" Hang on, friend, I'm about to flash some black light on a few hopeful road signs for you.

Climbing the Spiral Mountain

Several years ago, I met Kaye Briscoe King, a Christian counselor from Dallas, Texas. She introduced me to what I call the "Spiral Mountain." It got me off the roller coaster. Oh, I still experience some of the same kinds of highs and lows, but the lows are not as defeating anymore because I can see the opportunity in them. The Spiral can be explained with three simple facts. I view it as a journey up and around the mountain. At the top of the mountain is Christlike character, a noble quest to which God has called us. When we arrive at the destination we've grasped the Christlike qualities of love, peace, contentment, purity and more.

Credit: Spiral Mountain is adapted from "Journey: Wolfing into Wholeness: Body, Mind and Spirit," a booklet by Kaye Briscoe King of the Journey's Christian Counseling Center of Dallas. It has been modified for this book.

Do you ever feel like you've ruined the perfection God made when He first created you? Ever feel like your sin has marred God's pure creation? I have felt that way. In my quest to become Christlike, I feel ruined again and again by my sin and failure. But God's Word has a lot to say about the validity of those kinds of feelings.

You Were Not Born Pure

First, you were not born pure. Psalm 51:5 says, "Surely I have been a sinner from birth, sinful from the time my mother conceived me." How were you born? Sinful! You may have been innocent when you were born, but you were not born pure.

When it comes to sexual temptation, I know plenty of guys whose actions are anything but pure. They push the limit, and yet their technical virginity gives them this false sense of purity. Wrong! That's not purity. They may never have been pure. We were born sinful. That's why we need a Savior.

The moment we commit our lives to Christ and accept His precious blood as payment for our own sad, sinful nature, we begin the exciting journey toward becoming Christlike.

What's really exciting is that, with Christ, there's no more roller coaster. The new ride is far more exciting and far more productive than any roller coaster ever could be. Our new journey does not end where it begins.

. . . no more roller coaster . . . no more !

It's not unusual to experience what feels like ups and downs. But we actually are making progress on the Spiral Mountain. Elijah is one of my favorite Bible characters, because I can identify with his inconsistency. One event in his life shows how we move along Spiral Mountain.

In 1 Kings 18 we meet up with him as he comes out of hiding. He's been hiding from King Ahab and his nasty wife Jezebel, who was responsible for killing prophets like Elijah. Of course, Elijah hides to save his life. Meanwhile, the wicked king and queen set up a temple for Baal and one for Asherah.

One day, at the prompting of God, Elijah determines that it is time to put the king and queen in their places . . . and God in His rightful place. He calmly goes to see this vile enemy of God and himself. Elijah approaches the king, who immediately calls him a "troubler of Israel."

"Look who's talkin'!" Elijah shoots back.

He then boldly tells *the king* and his little prophets of false gods what to do. (Is that confidence or what?) He tells the king to bring the four hundred and fifty prophets of Baal and the four hundred prophets of Asherah to Mount Carmel. Who is Elijah to tell *them* what to do?

Up on the mountain, Elijah offers them the chance to see for themselves who is God . . . the God of Israel or Baal. In light of the recent drought, the prophet of God suggests that one of the gods might send rain if he's real and cares for the people. The people are all about that! Elijah doesn't just ask for rain, though. He invites the true God to strike His own altar with fire and consume the people's offering.

That's when the prophets of Baal get on board with all their hearts. I can imagine them standing there with slick, confident smiles across their faces.

Fire? That was Baal's specialty. Baal was the god of the sun. To honor him, they had an eternal flame right here in Israel. Fire was good. Very good.

You may know what happens next. The prophets of Baal put a sacrifice on their altar and for hours called on Baal. They yell, they dance, they even cut themselves in their wild frenzy . . . . nothing happens.

Then Elijah moves to the crumbling altar of God. He digs a deep trench, prepares the bull, cuts the wood and puts it into place; then he slaps the big dead animal on top of it all. Next he has the people fill the trench with water. The people do as Elijah says.

Then a hushed silence covers the mountain as even the prophets of Baal lay exhausted, watching the

man of God. There would be no wailing, no dancing, no gashing of flesh. Just a confident, well-spoken prayer uttered to an ever-living, ever-loving God.

"Whoosh!"

Fire thunders down from heaven and not only burns up the sacrifice and wood, but it dries up the water. That's amazing, but the most surprising part is that the fire actually decimated the rocks. Now, *that's* some fire.[1] Shortly, it begins to rain. In the course of a few hours, Elijah orchestrates one of the most famous victories in the Bible.

Wow! Great work, Elijah. Great faith, Elijah. But . . . When Ahab recounts the news to wicked Jezebel, the queen is not content that there is rain; she only hears that her beloved prophets have been killed. She issues a death threat to Elijah.

But Elijah is too confident in God's power to run from her, right? Wrong. Remember, we were not born perfect and that includes old Mr. Mighty Elijah. Elijah, who'd just led the way through one of the most amazing miracles in the Bible. In 1 Kings 19: 3–10, we read that the mighty prophet became depressed, full of self-pity, and had thoughts of suicide.

In His love, God continued to use Elijah; He took the prophet up Spiral Mountain in spite of Elijah's occasional slips—just as He takes you and me up that mountain.

Check out the second fact about the Spiral Mountain. You might not like this loop too much.

You Will Face Temptations Every Day

Second, you will face temptation in your life—every day and in every way. In Luke 17:1a, Jesus says, "Things that cause people to sin are bound to come." That's a promise I could do without. But the plain simple fact is this: You and I can be sure we will face temptation. You will face monsters like anger, depression, greed, and lust. As you journey up the mountain toward Christlike character, little evil monsters hang out just waiting to make you fail. You can count on it.

Now remember where Elijah is. Here's a guy who'd just had a real mountaintop experience—one you and I can only dream of experiencing. It is one of the greatest triumphs recorded in the Bible. He's just been on the mountain and is probably about ready to celebrate his fantastic Persian Gulfstyle victory and landslide vote of confidence for God. You'd think he'd never come down again, but come down he does and hard. Satan sends his little imps "depression" and "suicide" to do their work on Elijah. He runs off and hides. Afraid and lonely, he runs off and cries like a baby pleading with God to let him die.

Talk about cycling!

You and I *will* face temptation—those little monsters Satan sends our way to make us feel like we are hitting bottom.

Let's name just one—Lust. Each of us was born with Lust just hanging around. The dude was just sitting there waiting for us to get to him. When we do, he rears his ugly head—and you're checking in to the Smack Down Hotel.

One of three things will happen when you meet Lust.

1. **You'll breeze right past him with God's help.**
2. **He'll taunt and tease you into sin, but you get wise to his deception quite quickly.**
3. **You'll get stuck there with him for a long, long, long time.**

purity is not a fixed point

Hopefully, you'll make it past him pretty quickly. Ah, but one day, you notice (because you are walking in a spiral shape) that there he is again. He may be easier to identify and he might not seem as threatening, but there he is again. If you were like I used to be, he will make you feel like you are starting allllll over again every time you meet him. But that is not entirely true. There's good news. Just look at the third powerful truth.

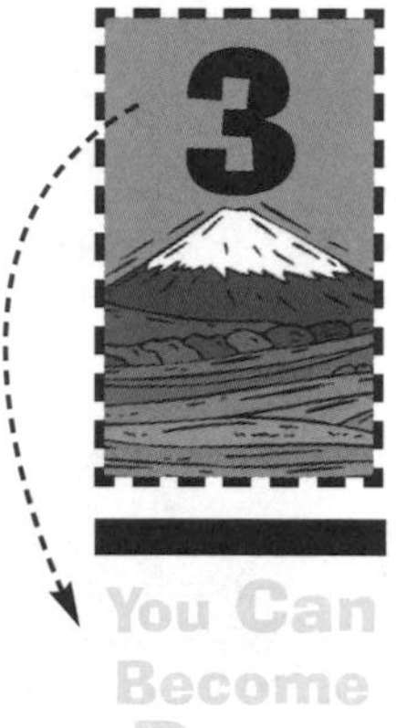

Third, you can become pure.

Thankfully, Elijah's story doesn't end at his showdown with suicide and depression. Instead Elijah became one of two men (the other is Enoch) that the Bible tells us escaped death as we know it! Second Kings 2: 11 says that "as [Elijah and Elisha] were walking along and talking together, suddenly a chariot of fire and horses of fire appeared and separated the two of them, and Elijah went up to heaven in a whirlwind."

Even though he had failure in his life, Elijah had progressed—he became so acceptable in God's sight that he would escape death. Elijah, just like you and me, was born sinful. And just like you and me, he had some dark moments of failure in his life. He probably felt like he was in the deep valley and had to start over, but in reality he was just on the side of that Spiral Mountain where the sun didn't shine. He was never back at the bottom. He was, in fact, moving closer to God, closer to the top of the mountain. Going through those tough times was a part of getting there. That's good news to a guy like me. How about you?

You can become pure, just like Philippians 2:15 says. God desires "that you may become blameless and pure."

In fact, meeting up with that guy lust—or anger, or depression, or greed—is a pretty good opportunity for you if you can handle it well.

C. S. Lewis illustrated the right approach in a tale he spun in The Great Divorce. A slimy red lizard clung to a certain ghost. The lizard taunted and teased that poor ghost, whispering great lies to him everyday. (Sound like lust?) The ghost tried to control the lizard, rather than live without him.

An angel appeared and offered to rid the ghost of the little lizard. The ghost understood that to be relieved of the lizard it would be necessary to kill it. The ghost wasn't quite sure he could live without the lizard. After all, he'd known him for so long.

The rationalizations began. The ghost thought he might tame the lizard or release it gradually. The angel insisted the gradual approach would not work, as this red lizard was a very good liar. It was either the death of the lizard or the defeat of the ghost.

Finally, the ghost gave the angel permission to remove the lizard. The lizard screamed as it was twisted from the shoulder it clung to. With one

great twist of the wrist, the angel sent the creature directly to the ground, where the impact broke its back. Then, an amazing thing happened. The ghost suddenly became a perfect man, and the limp, dead lizard was transformed into a very-much-alive silver and gold stallion. The new man leaped onto the great horse, and they rode off into the distance.

As Lewis explained, "What is a lizard compared with a stallion? Lust is a poor, weak, whimpering whispering thing compared with the richness and energy of desire which will arise when lust has been killed." [2]

"What is a lizard compared with a stallion? Lust is a poor, weak, whimpering whispering thing compared with the richness and energy of desire which will arise when lust has been killed."

C.S. LEWIS
The Great Divorce

How do you become pure? Chuck Swindoll says that every action either makes or unmakes character. By making right choices (or living righteously) even in the face of temptation like that evil dude Lust, you actually are afforded the great opportunity to develop purity. As you face the lust and make right choices to deny it and let Christ rid you of it, it is transformed into the Christlike character of purity.

When I had the Spiral explained to me, I suddenly realized that each time I met Lust, it was not a sin in itself *if* I did not give in to him. And, meeting him whether I gave in to him or not did not mean I was starting at the bottom of the valley of a roller coaster. Now I was traveling in a spiral. I may get stuck from time to time, but the totality of my experiences meant I was moving on in God's grace to become pure.

now I was traveling in a spiral

How energizing! Every stick I threw on those campfires at Word of Life was embraced by my Savior. Each one had been accepted with love. God knew I'd learned from my past year of facing lust. He knew that I'd grown closer as I walked up the Spiral Mountain, even if it often FELT to me as if I was starting at the bottom again.

Purity is not a fixed point. It is not a line I cross or don't cross. It's not something I gain or lose in one fell swoop. There will be moments of great victory. There will be moments of sad defeat. It's all a part of the process.

Purity is a process. It is the process of making right choices that transform temptation into purity. Embrace three truths:

1. **I was not born pure.**

2. **I will face temptations**—including the monster of Lust—perhaps over and over again, but that in itself is not a sin. Rather it is a chance to develop purity by talking to God and making right choices.

3. **I can become pure.**

Grasp that! It will save you a whole lot of confusion and "feelings" of defeat.

NOTES
1. See 1 Kings 18:30–39.
2. C.S. Lewis, *The Great Divorce* (New York: Macmillan, 1946), 104.

CHAPTER 7

the Covenant guarantees that Promise

"For this reason a man will leave his father and mother and be united to his wife, and the two will become one flesh." This is a profound mystery—but I am talking about Christ and the church.

EPHESIANS 5:31–32

the Covenant guarantees that Promise

Once when Dannah was speaking at a college campus, I saw her afterward talking with a young couple. He was a big, handsome guy with a clean, white smile. The kind of guy most of us love to hate. He looked at ease, in stark contrast to the girl beside him who looked completely embarrassed. I found out later that he'd come up to Dannah and said, "Hey, just want you to know that my girlfriend and I are really trying to set a good example about purity. We really love God and so we aren't having sex and we tell everyone we know so that they might be encouraged by our example. We tell them to try to do what we are doing and stick to just oral sex."

I hope that shocks you. It shocked me.

I think one of the reasons well-intentioned Christians give in to the temptation to have sex before marriage is that they do not understand sex. They are crying "Why wait?" The church fails to rise to answer that question. The rest of the world is eager to answer it. We hear messages like "Only intercourse is actually sex"; "Everybody is doing it"; "It's just a fun physical act"; and "Why do you have to miss the party?" The messages scream loudly at our value system. A truthful answer to the question "Why wait?" is hard to find.

How can I ever rearrange the meaning of sex in your mind? How can I ever rearrange it in my own?

What we are exposed to on a daily basis is destructive to the very meaning of sex as God created it to be. And, as we've talked about before, most of what you see and hear are lies. And we fall for them.

We are going deep now. We're going to define sex according to God's Word. I don't know how to make this effective in your mind since there's so much that distorts this truth, but we'll trust God to do that. It would help if you took a moment to unclutter your mind by asking God to prepare it for this truth.

Sexual Integrity Challenge

Normally, the "Sexual Integrity Challenge" comes at the end of the chapter. But I really think we need to do it right now as we approach a truly holy subject. I challenge you to get on your knees now and ask God to be your Teacher. Don't try to understand the truth of sexuality without asking God to help you overcome the lies of this world. Will you do that right now so you can understand the mystifying gift of sexuality?

A Covenant with God

To understand sex, you must understand the concept of covenant. Do you know what a covenant is? It's not a contract. It's not an agreement. A covenant is so much more than that. Every time God does something significant in Scripture, He presents it as a covenant. A biblical covenant can be recognized by three characteristics.

1. A covenant is an unbreakable bond.

What caused Jonathan to warn David, choosing a friend above his own father? They had a *covenant* relationship; that relationship superseded any other, even Jonathan's blood relationship with his dad. Oh, Jonathan loved his father—he ended up fighting to the death to protect his father's reign—but when David's life was endangered, the covenant relationship between Jonathan and David required him to warn his friend.[1]

Abraham is another good example of someone who had a covenant that was unbreakable. God made a covenant with Abraham that would ensure Abraham's descendants to be as plentiful as the stars in the universe . . . an amazing promise for an old man who had no children. What did God do to Abraham's name after the covenant was made? He changed it from Abram to Abraham.[2] Many Bible scholars believe that God was taking the H in his Hebrew name Yahweh and placing it within Abraham's name. His wife too, for Sarai became Sarah![3] It's also interesting that from that point on God refers to Himself and others refer to Him as the "God of Abraham." God and Abraham were bonded to one another in a permanent sense, having been re-identified to acknowledge the unending relationship.

2. A covenant is always sealed in blood.

Imagine being old, wrinkled, and very set in your ways when God shows up with the brilliant idea of . . . circumcision. Seriously, as a guy, just the sound of that word causes pain. You have to wonder if Abraham didn't think more than twice about that. And yet, as much as we know about Abraham's doubting God and His promise several times (laughing at the angels and having sex with Hagar to "help God out"), we don't have any record of hesitation about the idea of circumcision. This is because Abraham knew the power of the presence of blood. Every covenant in Scripture is sealed in blood.

Noah's rainbow was sealed in blood at the base through an animal sacrifice.

Old Testament characters had to shed animal blood to receive forgiveness of sins.

Christ shed His own blood to forgive us of our sins, wiping out Old Testament sacrifices.

Blood is present in every Biblical covenant. It is the blood that seals the covenant.

3. A covenant is followed by blessings in the form of an if/then agreement.

If Abraham would enter into the covenant of circumcision, *then* God would make his descendants like the stars of the universe. If Old Testament characters participated in animal sacrifice, *then* God would forgive their sins. If you and I embrace the blood of Jesus Christ as payment for our sins, *then* God forgives our sins and offers us eternal life.

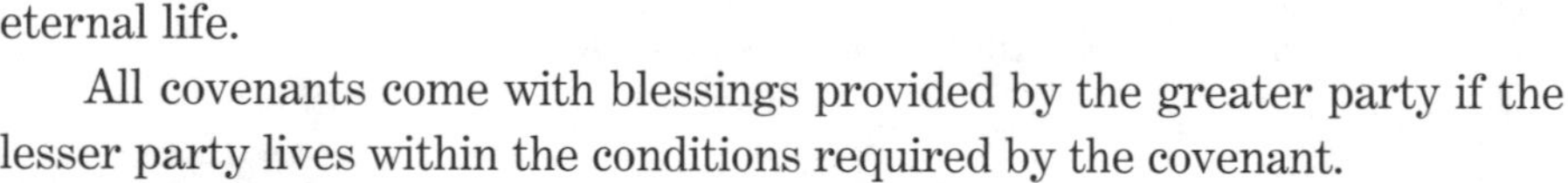

All covenants come with blessings provided by the greater party if the lesser party lives within the conditions required by the covenant.

A Sexual Covenant with God

So, how does the sexual relationship in marriage line up with the requirements of a biblical blood covenant? All three requirements of a blood covenant appear in the sexual covenant of marriage.

1. Sex is a covenant that is an unbreakable bond.

The Bible describes marriage as a covenant relationship. God refers to the marriage relationship throughout Scripture as a covenant. In several places, He alludes to His expectations that it should not be broken. For example, in Proverbs 2:17, He is grieved because a woman has "left the [husband] of her youth and ignored the covenant she made before God." God is grieved because He expected that marriage covenant like every other covenant to be honored as an *unbreakable* bond.[4]

The marriage relationship—sex—bonds us together emotionally, spiritually, and physically. When I took Dannah as my wife, she took my last name as hers. It is a sign, just like the change in Abraham's name, that we are bonded together. No matter where I go geographically, emotionally, spiritually, and mentally (and Dannah has good reason to wonder about that one), my wife is bonded to me. No matter where she goes, I am bonded to her.

Sex is a covenant that is an unbreakable bond.

2. Sex is a covenant that is sealed in blood.

When a virgin bride has sexual intercourse for the very first time, there is a small issue of blood. This occurs when the hymen, a thin membrane inside of her vagina, is stretched or torn. The hymen is the one tissue in the human body that medical science cannot quite figure out. They cannot identify any known purpose of the tissue. Every other tissue or hair has a specific biological function. I believe that God was checking off His list of requirements for covenants when He sealed the act of sexuality with blood through the hymen.

In Bible times this was taken very seriously. The bride and groom were presented with white linens on their wedding night. They were expected to provide proof of the young woman's virginity on those linens.

Sex is a covenant that is sealed in blood.

The Hymen

The hymen is named after the mythical god of marriage. It's a tiny little membrane that encompasses most of the lower opening of a young woman's vagina. The hymen has no known function and never grows back after is has been dilated or torn. Though a baby girl can be born without one and an adolescent girl can suffer a tear during rigorous exercise, this is rare. Even if a girl grew up without this membrane, it would not erase the physical portrait that the sexual union portrays of the spiritual truth of Christ and His beloved church.

Adapted from Dannah Gresh, And the Bride Wore White, 130.

3. Sex is a covenant that is followed by blessings in the form of an if/then agreement.

If we enjoy sex according to God's plan, *three* specific blessings will follow. Remember, God's plan requires us to wait until we are married to indulge our sexual desires—in any way whatsoever. But I think you will agree after looking at these fantastic blessings that there is some great motivation to wait.

We will look at all three in the next chapter. For now, let's consider the first blessing: Sex is a spiritual portrait that enhances intimacy. (OK, we aren't starting with the most enjoyable of the sexual blessings—pleasure—but stick with me and we will get there.)

Sex is not just physical. It is very emotional, very spiritual. When two people who have never had sex enter into the marriage covenant . . . no one else is in that place they go to. No one else knows that person so well, not just physically, but emotionally and spiritually. The result is an intimacy that is far more than just physical.

Ephesians 5:31–32 says, "For this reason a man will leave his father and mother and be united to his wife, and the two will become one flesh. This is a profound mystery—but I am talking about Christ and the church." Whoa! One second Paul is taking about sex and the next about the great mysterious relationship between Christ and the church? Yes!

sex is . . . very emotional, very spiritual

At the last supper Christ said, "If I go and prepare a place for you, I will come back." That zooms right over our heads. It has no meaning to us, but to the disciples it was a clear picture.

You see, in Christ's day, when it was time for a young Jewish guy to become engaged to his bride-to-be, a very specific order of events began to take place. First, the groom and his family had to prove he would be worthy of providing for the girl by giving some sort of payment. Sometimes the payment was a cow or two. Sometimes if they had no things of value they could offer a few years of labor. (Remember, Jacob offered seven years of labor for Rachel. Poor guy. Must've had it bad!)

Then, after the payment was made, the guy had to go prepare a home. This could take months or years. He had to have the materials and time to build. He would usually add a room onto his dad's house. Sometimes he built his own house if he could afford it. As the construction was complete, the excitement grew, because the *moment* it was finished the groom and his buddies marched through the streets whooping and hollering as they moved toward the bride's home. No matter when it was—noon or three in the morning—he would return for his faithfully waiting bride for he had "paid the price" and "prepared a place" for her.

See the picture? Do you see Christ paying for us just like the young man paid for the girl of his dreams? Do you see Christ ascending into heaven to "prepare a place for us" just as the young man went to build a home for his bride? And one day our Savior will return again when we least expect it, just like the young man returned for his bride as soon as his home was ready for her.

The intimacy of sex is so intense that it is compared to the unfathomable love of Christ for His church. This is significant. You see, God's Word tells us that for every great spiritual truth, He offers us a physical example of it on earth. My friend, sex is the great physical example of Christ's intense love for you and me!

Sex is separated and exalted as the portrait of the greatest spiritual truth that you and I know. There is a Savior. He loves us passionately. He paid the price for our sins on the cross. He has gone to prepare a place for you. He will come again to get you and take you there. That's powerful!

What motivation for Satan to distort this truth in your life! How he wants you to water down the intensity of sex so you cannot understand the passion Christ has for you! He wants to make your parents' marriage a broken example of this powerful portrait! He wants to ruin this gift for you!

Don't let him. **Stand strong. Protect the truth.**

OK, all of this has been pretty heady, but I need you to understand the heavenly purpose of sex. Sex really is out of this world! Know that truth. Now, let's get on with those blessings as we bring sex down to earth!

NOTES
1. See 1 Samuel 18:1–4; 19:1–7; 20:1–42.
2. See Genesis 12:1–3; 15:1–21; 17:1–9.
3. See Genesis 17:15–16.
4. Ezekiel 16:8; Malachi 2:14–16.

CHAPTER 8

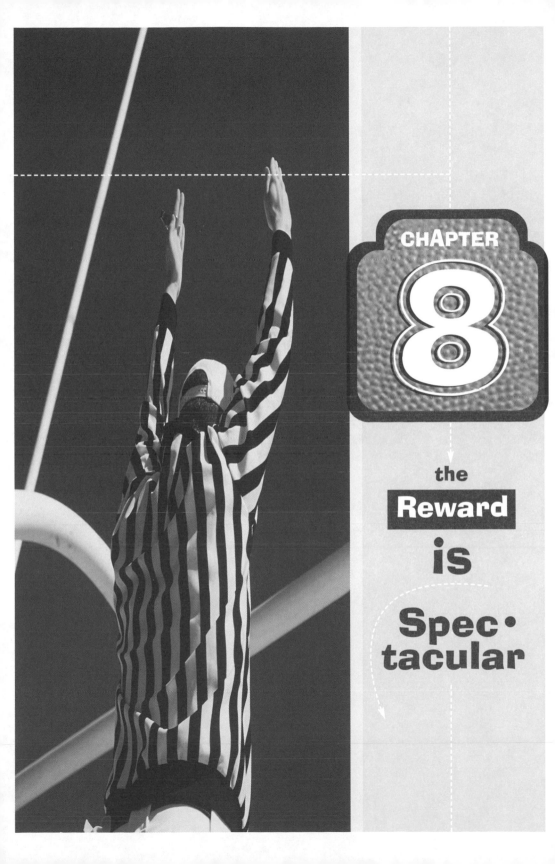

the Reward is Spec•tacular

May you rejoice in the wife of your youth. . . . May you be ever captivated by her love!"

PROVERBS 5:18–19

the Reward is Spec•tacular

You may be saying, *OK, all that heavenly stuff is great and it's very eye-opening and a little motivating, but I've got to live with these physical desires here on earth.* Hang in there. God's got that under control. Let's just see how He brings the great gift of sexuality down to earth.

We just learned that sex is a covenant and a big part of covenant is the blessings or benefits that follow if that covenant is enjoyed according to God's plan. The covenant of sexuality has three great benefits. (Stick with me on the first two benefits. They're hard for us guys to grasp but, I'm saving the fun one for last . . . and don't you dare skip ahead!).

Benefit Number One:

Sex Is a Spiritual Portrait that Enhances Intimacy

My home church in State College recently had me speak to our teens at a purity retreat. What a weekend! To explain these three benefits to our youth group, I had some very cool couples in our church talk about their own marriages. Youth pastor and worship band leader Jonathan Weibel and his wife, Suzy, tackled the subject of intimacy.

Jonathan is one of the most spiritually intimate guys I have ever met. He goes deep right away. No superficiality. He gets to the core. As a result, his ministry is powerful and effective. As he talked about intimacy that day, he shifted back and forth in his seat for a few minutes and then just spilled his guts. **"I gotta be honest with you. I don't really get this.** I can't grasp it. It's too huge for me. The idea of being totally intimate with Suzy is really hard for me." Suddenly, all the guys were right there with him. The teens and the married mentors sat there with their heads bobbing up and down. I understood. In fact, it made me feel so relieved to know he was in the same boat with me. I don't expect you to get this fully, but give it a try. I'm still trying.

> **I understood that day God said it was good**

When sex is pure, it brings you to a new level of oneness, the level God speaks of in Ephesians 5:31–32. "A man will leave his father and mother and be united to his wife, and the two will become one flesh. This is a profound mystery." The intimacy between you and your one-day wife should be so intense that it is *mysterious*.

Something that helps me get this into my head is the idea that Adam was alone before Eve was created. Here's Adam hangin' in the garden, wearin' nothing but a smile. He was sinless. He had no guilt or shame or fear to deal with. He didn't have to work. *And yet,* God looked at him and realized that it wasn't good for him to be alone. Everything else in the garden was good . . . everything. But it was not good that Adam was alone.

Alone? God Himself was walking and talking with Adam. Alone? How could he be alone? God could have used Himself to fill Adam's void, but he didn't. Instead, Adam wouldn't be complete until God created Eve. His loneliness would not be voided until Eve was present.

If you think naked women look good, imagine what Adam must have experienced when he looked at Eve. He'd never seen a woman, let alone a *naked* woman. What man could dream up something as fabulous as a woman's body? Adam takes a nap one day and when he opens his eyes, there she is. He's lost a rib but gained a companion who's a perfect ten. Nice trade, huh? Now, Adam was also nude at the time, yet there was no shame. (P. S. Don't try this at home). Pretty interesting, huh? That day, as Adam looked upon his new naked companion, he was complete.

That day God said it was good.

There was no shame. Adam was not alone.

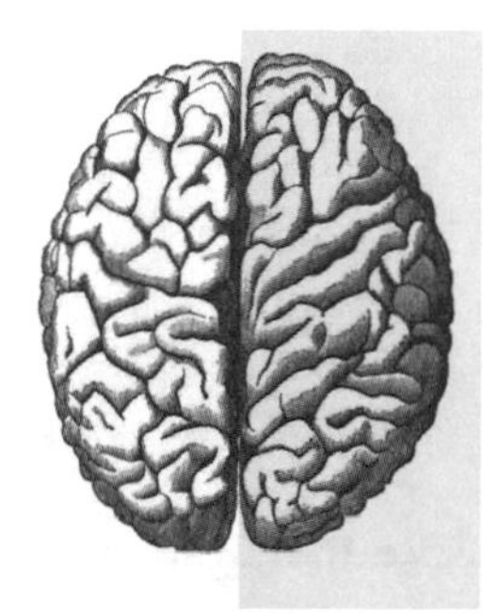

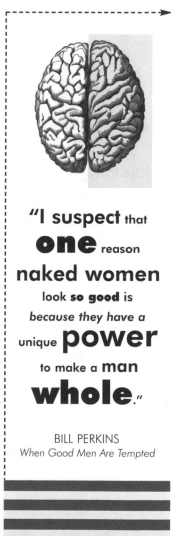

"I suspect that one reason naked women look so good is *because they have a* unique power to make a man whole."

BILL PERKINS
When Good Men Are Tempted

Recently Dannah and I participated in a marriage conference where Dr. Joseph Stowell, president of Moody Bible Institute, spoke. He talked about how when things are OK with his wife in every way—and he was brave enough to include sexuality—it did not matter what happened at work. He still felt OK. Problems could arise that might seem overwhelming, he said, but if things were OK at home, life was OK. On the other hand, if things didn't go so well at home the night before a big day at work, all the kudos and successes his career could bring him would never make that day OK.

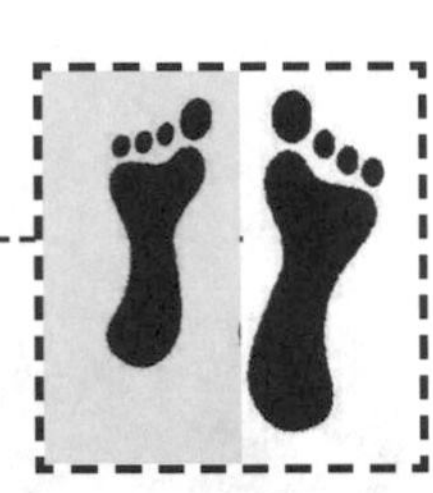

Take It a Step Further

Tim and Beverly LaHaye surveyed more than 3,300 Christian couples to learn about their sex lives. According to them, the couples who prayed together regularly were more than 10 percent more likely to have a "very happy/above average" sex life than those who did not pray together.[1] Why? Because God loves to be in the very center of a vibrant marriage relationship and He blesses that with the great physical gift of sexual satisfaction.

How could that be? He is emotionally bonded to his wife.

It's actually much more complex than that, but Stowell was experiencing the emotional impact sex has on a married person. In contrast, sex outside of marriage usually will create very opposite feelings of shame and embarrassment. Sex outside of commitment can actually ruin a relationship. It gets in the way of the emotional and spiritual parts of the relationship and creates discomfort, shame, and a lack of intimacy. Within the marriage bed, however, it motivates and excites us. It releases our potential as individuals and as a married couple. It makes us want to love emotionally.

It does for Dannah and me. It makes us want to talk. We find ways to do special things for each other. I find myself wanting to take her out for lunch the next day just so I can be with her again. And she makes my favorite foods or goes out of the way to help me with a project when we've been physically intimate. It's a warm and wonderful cycle of loving. We love physically, which makes us love emotionally, which makes us love physically, which makes us . . . well, you get the idea. It's a lot of fun and it's very fulfilling.

Don't risk marring that. Sex enhances intimacy in our marriages if we wait.

Benefit Number Two:
Sex Creates Life

Genesis 1:28 issues an early command for us to populate the earth . . . to make babies! Imagine, God not only lets us have sex, He *commands* us to have sex. Wow! That's the first blessing of sexuality that Scripture addresses.

The girls have it in the bag as far as understanding this one early on. My wife laughs when she says there is this saying among some girls that they want to "get married, have babies, and then Jesus can come back!" They get it. Maybe they understand because they will carry the child within them, but it takes us men to get it there. We need to try to understand this awesome gift.

When Dannah and I first discovered that she was pregnant, I was thrilled. Every moment from that point on was a celebration!

I will never forget the morning of July 21, 1990. I snuck out for a quick haircut. When I returned, Dannah had a suitcase beside her and said, "It's time!" Poor Dannah! It wasn't her most comfortable moment, but I had to take a minute to express myself. I jumped on the bed like a five-year-old. I ran through our little duplex doing dances usually seen only in the end zone after Super Bowl touchdowns. I ended my celebration by spiking teddy bears in the nursery as if they were footballs. I simply couldn't contain myself. It was an awesome moment.

get married and have babies

The incredible gift of creating life is the most God-like thing you or I can do. Certainly, it's been done outside of marriage time and time again. But the gift is so amazing, it deserves to be unmarred and undistracted by bad timing.

If we wait to have sex until we are married, then we make babies with great celebration.

Benefit Number Three: Sex is Sheer Pleasure

If the girls get the last blessing, *we* get this one. That's why it can be so hard for us to wait—we are wired to be visually stimulated and to initiate sex. We are fully aware of how fun and fantastic it can be.

Andy and Janet Mylin, two friends who are youth leaders, once participated in a youth group's panel discussion on sex. Janet told the teens that her husband and she are like "each other's *sexual theme parks*." Andy just nodded proudly and offered a big toothy grin. Then she explained: "Everywhere we go, we get to take each other," she said.

"Even when there's nothing to do, hey, it beats Disneyland." Andy smiled and paused. "Well, there's always *something* to do!"

They enjoy each other. They have fun . . . much more than they would at a theme park!

Proverbs 5:18–19 says, "May your fountain be blessed, and may you rejoice in the wife of your youth. A loving doe, a graceful deer—may her breasts satisfy you always, may you be ever captivated by her love."

"May her breasts satisfy you always." I like that verse.

But you have to look back a verse, to verse 18: It's one *wife* . . . the wife of your youth. There will come a day when you can be fully satisfied by your wife's breasts . . . always.

If you translated that verse more accurately from the original Hebrew text, that last phrase, "may you be ever captivated by her love" would read, "may you be intoxicated by her sex." Get the picture, guys? She is so fantastic. The experience is so fantastic that you are *intoxicated* by nothing but the thought of sex with her. Wow!

This is a good time to bring up something. Sex *is* fun, so why does God withhold it from us?

In the book of Deuteronomy, God says basically that He knows we are going to wonder why He has placed guidelines for living upon us. He doesn't want us to wonder what they are all about, so He says right out that the purpose of them is to make us "prosper." He wants us to prosper . . . that includes sexually. He doesn't ask us to wait to have sex to torture us. He knows that if we wait, it will be far more fantastic.

Social science proves this today. In a landmark study of sexual practices entitled "Sex in America," the authors concluded, "People who reported being the most physically pleased and emotionally satisfied [with sex] were the married couples." They also reported that "the lowest rates of satisfaction were among men and woman who were neither married nor living with someone—the very group[s] thought to be having the hottest sex." Furthermore, "physical and emotional satisfaction started to decline when people had more than one sexual partner."[2] Science today proves what God said thousands of years ago. When we wait to have sex with one woman, it is more fantastic!

it's about waiting to have it right

fun sex is blessed by God

Sometimes Satan tries to make us feel like we are missing the party by waiting to have sex. It's not true. Abstinence is about not having sex. Purity and sexual integrity is about waiting to have it right. It's about going to the big party. It's about having total, free, and fun sex because it is blessed by God.

On the contrary, those who fail to wait tend to face obstacles in learning to have fun in their married sex lives. In *What Hollywood Won't Tell You About Sex, Love and Dating*, Greg Johnson says that he and his wife were virgins by God's grace on their wedding day, but they had been physical up to a certain point. Because of that sexual activity, they had trained her body to get to a certain point and then stop. So, when they got married, it took them several years of reconditioning to teach her body to enjoy sexual intimacy and get to the point where they were blessed by the fantastic fun of sex. [3]

I am not saying that sex outside of marriage is not fun. Would we need a book like this if it wasn't? I am saying with certainty that sex outside of marriage is a substitute for the real depth of pleasure that can be experienced when sex is protected.

God wants you to have a fantastic, fun sexual relationship that's more than you can even imagine. Don't miss out on the fun by settling for a substitute.

If we wait to have sex, then it's a blast!

Sexual Integrity Challenge

I get frustrated with many in the church who won't talk about sex. I am calling on you to be a part of changing that. Speak boldly. Be ready to be a bold example of sexual integrity for those behind you that need a good example and those ahead of you who were not.

I want you to just start with a simple task right now. Imagine that a close friend of your has just walked up to you and said, "What's the big deal about sex? Don't you get it? You're missing the party. What are you waiting for!?" What would you say? Grab your journal and just write a quick note to that friend right now. Someone just might ask you a question a lot like that one day. I want you to be ready with an answer!

NOTES

1. Tim and Beverly LaHaye, *The Act of Marriage* (Grand Rapids: Zondervan, 1976), 209.
2. Robert T Michael, John H. Gagnon, Edward O. Laumann, and Gina Kolata, *Sex in America* (New York: Warner Books, 1994), 124.
3. Greg Johnson and Susie Shellenberger, *What Hollywood Won't Tell You About Sex, Love and Dating* (Ventura, Calif.: Regal, 1994), 17–18.

Part 3: Seven Strategies for Success

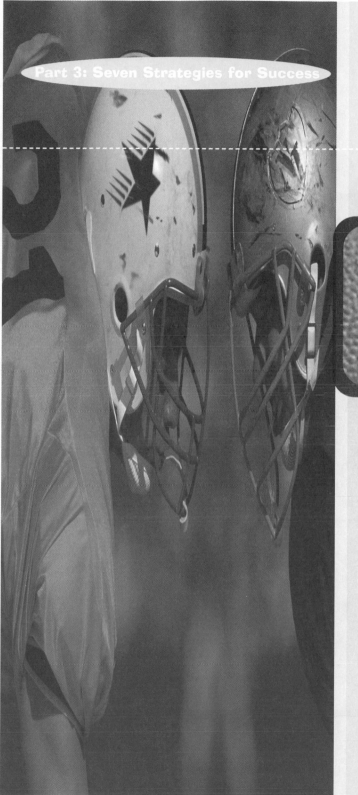

Strategy #1

maintain your Brain

[Let] there be no going along with the crowd, the empty-headed, mindless crowd. They've refused for so long to deal with God that they've lost touch not only with God but with reality itself. They can't think straight anymore. Feeling no pain, they let themselves go in sexual obsession, addicted to every sort of perversion.

EPHESIANS 4:17–19 *(The Message)*

CHAPTER 9

Strategy #1

maintain your Brain

The night started out innocent. I was home alone with a lapful of junk food and the remote control. I had an entire night of Monday night football ahead of me . . . or so I thought.

At halftime it happened.

I picked up the remote control and surfed my way through the channels.

Before I knew it, I was in Florida experiencing *Spring Break Uncensored.* And uncensored it was. My curiosity was piqued by the confessions of roommates. It was staged and stupid. Then came something called the "shot-glass quick-draw," which couldn't have been less tempting to me, but it was hilarious to see guys and girls drunk as skunks trying to walk straight on the sand. The finale was the big male/female swimsuit-switching contest. I couldn't believe my eyes. Was it possible these coeds were actually swapping swimsuits on national television? These guys were having some good time.

Welcome to the world of prime-time MTV.

I never did catch the final score of the game.

X-X-X-X-O-O-O-O

I'm not the only Christian guy who's fallen prey to unexpected temptation on a Monday night. *Focus on the Family's Boundless* web magazine recently posted an article entitled "Mainstreaming Porn." Author Roberto Rivera admitted:

> **While channel surfing** during the commercials on 'Monday Night Football,' I came across the offerings of VH-1. . . . The show was entitled "Porn to Rock." . . . The show chronicled the musical aspirations of two 'adult' film stars . . . [One] had made more than 100 films, told VH-1 that record producers had approached her. Why? It certainly wasn't her voice . . . [1]

Hey, admit it. You've seen some of this stuff, too. You don't have to turn to MTV, VH-1 or HBO to find it. I can *promise* you it'll be there. It's everywhere.

It is not hard to run right out of bounds of God's playing field. Sometimes the crowd around us is actually cheering us on. It's never a good idea to listen to the roar of the crowd. Instead, we should pay attention to the rules God gives. If we want to be successful in life, including in sexual integrity, we must play by God's rules.

we must play by God's rules

Have You Lost Your Mental Virginity?

Sometimes we go out of bounds not physically but mentally. We guys are tempted to give in to the corruption of our minds. It has become normal and accepted for us

Standing Alone

It does no good to play offense; that is, removing the culture from your life. You also have to play defense, protecting the decisions you've made. Sometimes that might seem pretty impossible. I'm sure for Baltimore Colt R.C. Owens it seemed that way when the Washington Redskins were lined up to kick a field goal. What could be done? Owens, a former basketball star and high jumper for the University of Idaho, had an idea. As Washington's Bob Khayat lined up to kick a 40-yard field goal, Owens planted himself in front of the ten-foot-high crossbar. And you can imagine, he was all alone back there . . . far from the rest of the team. He was separated. I can imagine there was some fury amidst the Baltimore fans as they looked at the seemingly misplaced Colt. The kick went up. So did Owens. He leapt high and swatted the perfect kick away just as it was about to cross the field goal. The date was December 8, 1962, and today it remains the only field goal blocked from 40 yards!

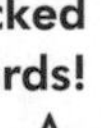

to expose ourselves to visual sex. We make "popular" choices when it comes to our everyday lives. Have you ever:

- **Gone to an R-rated movie that had a sex scene?**
- **Laughed at the sexual innuendos on one of the most popular TV shows?**
- **Glanced through a magazine filled with sexually charged advertising?**
- **Stumbled onto an Internet porn site with nudity?**

If you answered "yes" to any (or all) of these, I have news for you. You've compromised your mental virginity! I realize that sounds pretty harsh, so stick with me while I explain.

When we expose ourselves to stuff like that, we begin to lose touch with reality. Ephesians 4 says "[Let] there be no going along with the crowd, the empty-headed, mindless crowd. They've refused for so long to deal with God that *they've lost touch not only with God but with reality* itself. They can't think straight anymore. Feeling no pain, they let themselves go in sexual obsession, addicted to every sort of perversion."[2]

They can't think straight anymore!

Can you? **Can I?**

The crowd presses, pushing us along with a strength greater than we fully realize. The pop culture of today has "refused for so long to deal with God that they've lost touch with . . . God,"—and "with reality itself."

We think we are above it all. We think we can handle it without actually letting ourselves get out of control, but can we? I say we can't. The body and mind respond uncontrollably and unavoidably to the environment.

It's simple science! Our sexual organs are activated by the body's autonomic nervous system (ANS). This system is not controlled by the will, but by the environment. For example, let's imagine you're sixteen. (Maybe you are!) Let's imagine your dad

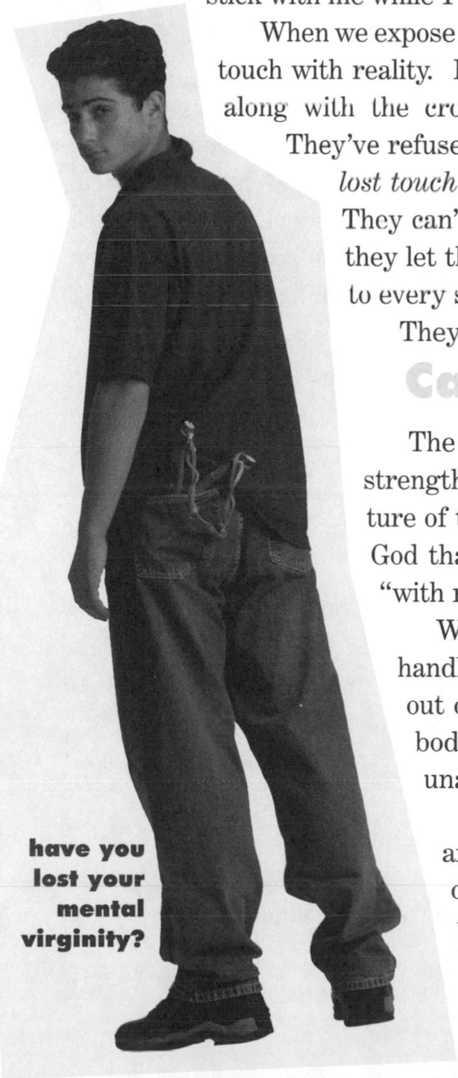

have you lost your mental virginity?

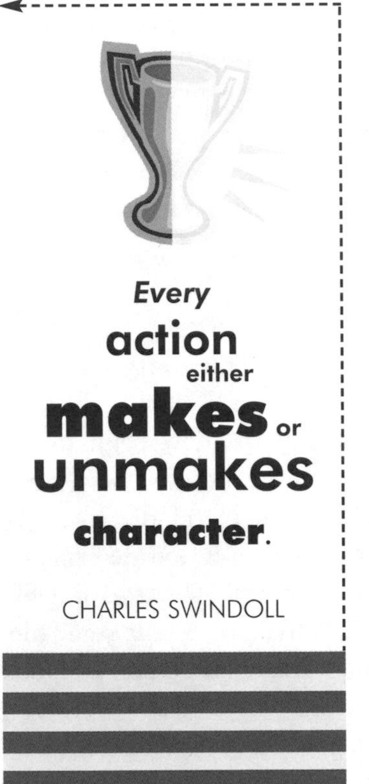
Every
action
either
makes or
unmakes
character.
CHARLES SWINDOLL

told you not to drive the car, but you did and—you had a fender bender. Back home, you sit sweating it out when suddenly you hear Dad returning for the day. How does your body respond? You might experience a rapid pulse, more sweat, and perhaps even heavy breathing. You might get a sick feeling in your stomach.

You cannot control these things by choice. It's your ANS in action. You are scared out of your wits, and your body is telling you about it! Now, how you act when Dad comes around the corner—take a quick hike up to the bedroom to hide or stand firm to tell the truth—is entirely up to you. But your body's initial response was not controlled by your will but by the environment.

how does your body respond?

Sexual arousal works the same way. Things in the environment—what we see, what we hear, and what we smell—work together to tell the brain that the time is right for sexual arousal. At that time, the brain sends chemicals through your body. Your pulse changes, you experience a change in body temperature, and your penis begins to become erect. You have been aroused! You may not have willfully created these reactions in your body, but the environment created them.

Just as in our car-wreck scenario where you had a choice with what you did with the fear when Dad came home, you have a choice with what you will do when you initially become sexually aroused. (But don't rely on it. An aroused guy doesn't usually listen to his conscience.) You can get outta there or think about something to diminish the response. But it's way too easy to let your imagination run with it as you fantasize about what could come next.

I'll admit it. It's absolutely impossible to completely avoid all the billboards, the scantily clad women walking by you, and just plain fantastic-looking girls that create a hint of arousal. When you run into that kind of temptation, you can call it enticement. Enticement is "passive temptation." It's passive in the sense that you did not realize that you'd be weakened by walking past that shoe store with the poster of a girl wearing, of course, shoes . . . and not much else. You get the idea. You don't know temptation is around the corner. You passively walked into it. That's enticement.

enticement is "passive" temptation

But be warned, my friend. Enticement is dangerous! Exposing yourself to temptation—whether surfing the Internet unfiltered or just watching a sexually charged prime-time comedy with some buddies—is inviting sin. Since every action either makes or unmakes character, yielding to temptation plants one more seed that gives birth to future temptations.

It's like planting dandelions.

Have You Been Planting Dandelions?

The way you keep dandelions out of your yard is to eliminate them from your yard (by the roots) *but also by establishing a perimeter outside your yard.* I've seen so many immaculate yards with dandelions all around the edges because the seeds from the neighbor's yard blew into their own.

That's what I see happening to us as Christians. We don't want to be too prudish. So we go with all our friends to see that hilarious R movie even though there's a raw nude scene. We watch the most popular TV sitcoms even though sex is the main focus of almost every joke. And we surf the net unfiltered and visit questionable chat rooms.

remember Samson? he had a very bad hair day

We do these things because they are common and accepted. We do them because it would be lonely not to participate in the lunchroom conversation. We do these things because it can be uncomfortable to be separated. But we better be careful—we must overcome the crowd or face being thrown for a loss.

Remember good ol' Samson from the Bible? He was uncomfortably separated. At first, he wanted to be pleasing to God, and he was. By the age of forty he'd managed to keep his long-hair weapon a secret and in doing so had crushed the Philistines, and Israel ruled for twenty years. He was the spiritual leader of Israel. He was on top of the world. He'd accomplished it all.

If only he could have stayed separated.

But he became bored.

In his boredom, he remembered the place of *his* enticement—Timnah. In his hours of boredom, he became preoccupied with his memories of the Philistine women, and his fantasy life took over. He soon traveled to the city of Gaza. Like some of us, maybe he was planning to "just look." He was moving back into the flow of the crowd.

In those days, "just looking" meant actual flesh. There was no Internet. There were no magazines. Just real women in what we would call red-light districts. Off he went and . . . well, you know the rest of the story. He had sex with Delilah and the power of that sexual relationship causes him to give up his secret. Eventually a Philistine cut his hair, and Samson's God-given strength disappeared. He ended up tied to the temple pillars with his eyes blinded. His boredom led to a full-fledged sin that ruined his life.

"**Choosing** to be **pure** means *giving up* **something** you enjoy. It means **embracing** discomfort and **boredom**."

BILL PERKINS
When Good Men Are Tempted

It all started when Samson compromised the distance and difference. He started out just allowing the dandelions of others to be near him, and he ended up with an overgrowth of nasty weeds. That was all that was left to his story.

In our lives, we *must* establish solid boundaries so that casual contact doesn't allow seeds of future temptation to be planted. These boundaries make it harder for the pull of the crowd to overcome you. It's harder to come into contact with the enticement when you are separated from it.

we *must* establish boundaries

That's where the elimination of a lot of common pastimes becomes important.

Is that distance there in your life? Ask yourself some tough questions.

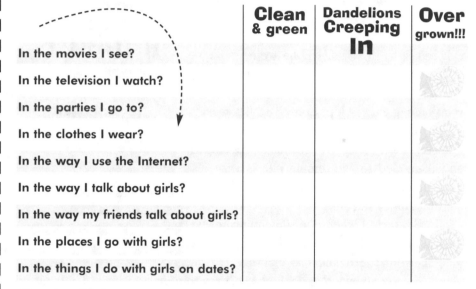

Sexual Integrity Challenge

How's your life's yard looking?
Evaluate whether you have clean boundaries in your life. Evaluate your life's yard in nine areas by putting a check mark in the appropriate column.

	Clean & green	Dandelions Creeping In	Over grown!!!
In the movies I see?			
In the television I watch?			
In the parties I go to?			
In the clothes I wear?			
In the way I use the Internet?			
In the way I talk about girls?			
In the way my friends talk about girls?			
In the places I go with girls?			
In the things I do with girls on dates?			

Overall I:

____Am doing well. I'm not planting dandelions as a common practice.

____Am waaaay too close to it all, and I need to establish some new guidelines.

____Am a dandelion greenhouse, and I need to get some help to make some changes.

Living a life of sexual integrity requires you to hear God's Word above the din of the crowd's roar. Sexual purity has been defined as "the control and direction of sexual powers and impulses in accordance to the law and purpose of God."[3] Control! Direct! Are you controlling the level of enticement in your life? Are you directing the course of your sexual powers and impulses according to God's laws? Or are you just going along with the mindless, empty-headed crowd?

control! direct!

You might not yet think it is important to separate yourself, but let me assure you it is. Just look at the next stage of sexual sin. Enticement is accompanied by a nasty little friend!

Autobiography in Five Short Chapters

Chapter 1

I walk down the street.
There is a deep hole in the sidewalk.
I fall in.
I am lost . . . I am hopeless.
It isn't my fault.
It takes forever to find a way out.

Chapter 2

I walk down the same street.
There is a deep hole in the sidewalk.
I pretend I don't see it.
I fall in again.
I can't believe I am in the same place.
But . . . it isn't my fault.

Chapter 3

I walk down the same street.
There is a deep hole in the sidewalk.
I see it is there.
I still fall in...it's a habit.
My eyes are open.
I know where I am.
It is my fault.
I get out immediately.

Chapter 4

I walk down the same street.
There is a deep hole in the sidewalk.
I walk around it.

Chapter 5

I walk down another street.[4]

NOTES

1. Roberto Rivera, "Mainstreaming Porn" *Boundless*, 9 January 2001; accessed 18 January 2001 at www.family.org; click *Boundless* (under "collegians," then "Boundless Columnists". Also available at www.boundless.org/2000; click "Boundless Columnists."
2. Ephesians 4:17–19 *The Message;* italics added.
3. Francis Foulkes, *Ephesians: New Testament Commentaries* (Grand Rapids: InterVarsity,1989), 148.
4. Portia Nelson, *There's a Hole in My Sidewalk* (Hillsboro, Ore.: Beyond Words Publishing 1993), 2–3. Used by permission.

CHAPTER 10

Strategy #2:

trigger · lock your cycle

Chapter 10

Strategy #2

trigger·lock your cycle

Dannah Barker. Here she was right beside me at Wittenburg Library. We came here a lot. In the crowded hush of the library, we felt like we were alone, but we were safely under the watchful eyes of those around us.

She was the girl I'd been waiting for, yet my attitude toward her had been lacking. I didn't spoil her or dress up for her or try to impress her. It wasn't natural and something wasn't right.

The basic, plain fact was that I didn't love God or myself. I didn't love myself because I'd lost the one thing I was most proud of—my character. I scratched out some thoughts in my journal as Dannah worked on her studies.

Dannah sensed my heavy spirit. We began to talk. The conversation was one I had not been prepared for nor did I think it was one I would ever have.

"Whatcha thinkin' about?" she innocently prodded.

We sat there eye-to-eye. My heart pounded. My hands sweated. She calmly fired questions. I didn't know that I wanted to answer them, but I heard my voice overriding my fear. I saw her face become serious and sad.

She went deeper. She asked more. She listened somewhat naively. She dug deeper into my life than anybody ever had.

It scared me. There was a crack in the wall. Worse yet, I'd just let someone see that there WAS a wall there.

"Television evangelist Jim Bakker went down this week," I told Dannah. "He was caught having a sexual affair with a secretary. That could be me."

Though I hadn't been sinning at that level, lust ruled my life. I knew it was controlling much of my life.

"In a twisted way," I said, "my allegiance to Christ is strong enough to keep me in bed rather than to speak out for Him and be found a hypocrite. Yet my faith isn't strong enough to overcome this besetting sin."

I sensed the Lord speaking to me—through Dannah's questions. I'd have given almost anything to be free of my sin . . . free to truly love her. I sensed that as long as I was giving in to lust, I would not be able to love. I just didn't know how to stop it. It always seemed to be the same thing that pulled me down.

←-------XXXX-OOOO-------→

OK, here's the hard part. You bought this book to figure out the real answers to beating temptation. Success means conditioning and sacrifice. As they say in football, "If you wanna run with the big dogs, you'd better get off the porch." So, step in and be a man.

There are lots of areas in which we find ourselves enticed. Let's continue to look at an obvious area of distraction—entertainment. For years I watched what I wanted, but I can't do that anymore. I've seen the pattern of enticement when I've watched certain movies or even prime-time TV shows. Take the show *Friends*. I love that show's staging, writing, and characters, but every episode is full of sexual messages that erode my faith. I can't watch that! MTV's *Real World* is a good example of a TV show that doesn't really show any sex, but makes light of it in just about every episode. Much of TV has an element of arousal or at least a desensitizing quality that makes sexual immorality more normal in your mind.

The first time you run into that tingly sensation that invites you to exercise your sexual desires, it's just enticement. But be warned; enticement can quickly become more.

step in and be a man

Working Out Your Muscle Memory

It's like what athletes call "muscle memory." Many players whose muscles have been out of commission for a period of time report retraining that muscle at an accelerated rate upon returning to the practice field. Science calls this a phenomenon, because it cannot quite be explained medically, but the fact is that the muscle does "remember."

Motion picture soundtracks are a good example of how our brains develop muscle memory. Remember the soundtrack of *Jaws*? Even though the theme is played by the same instruments that might perform the Star Spangled Banner, the Jaws theme stirs up fearful visuals and unsettling emotions. (Believe me! It won't be the theme song for Daytona Beach anytime soon.) The *Mission Impossible* theme is the same way, but it offers thrilling excitement. The theme from *Rocky* will pump you up for a good fight! Our minds are definitely programmable.

Watch enough sexually explicit movies and you'll begin to believe that everywhere guy meets girl from across a crowded room, they're bound to be tumbling into bed within fifteen minutes. It becomes programmed into your mind. And the next time a great looking girl innocently looks at you from across the room, your mind is headed to places it has no business being. Your muscle memory has been triggered! You know that feeling, don't you? Most guys do.

you know that feeling, don't you?

You need to carefully examine your life to identify your muscle memory triggers. While enticement is passive temptation, *triggers are "repeated, expected temptations."* You've been there before and you *know* it was tempting.

I think I can help you identify the triggers in your life. First let's start by isolating the times when you are most vulnerable. Ted Roberts asks these questions in his book *Pure Desire*. Take a moment to circle your answers.

what day! of the week am I most tempted?

Monday
Tuesday
Wednesday
Thursday
Friday
Saturday
Sunday

what time! of the day am I most tempted?

Morning
Lunchtime
Afternoon
Dinner
Early Evening
Late Evening

where! am I tempted the most?

Home
School
Work
Around Town
In My Car
Other

what! is my emotional status at the time I am most tempted?

Confident/Free
Sad/Depressed
Angry/Upset
Rejected/Alone

SOURCE: TED ROBERTS, PURE DESIRE, 118.

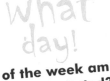

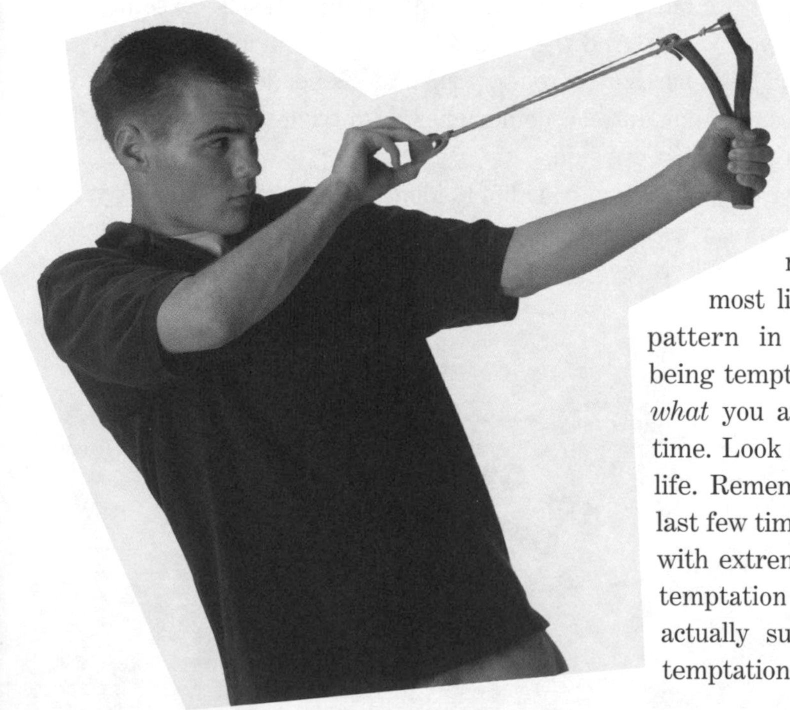

surfing the net
kissing
movies with nudity

OK, now you have most likely identified a pattern in *when* you are being tempted. Let's look at *what* you are doing at that time. Look carefully at your life. Remember back to the last few times you struggled with extreme mental sexual temptation or maybe you actually succumbed to the temptation and acted out by having sex in some form with a girl or by masturbating. What were your muscle memory triggers . . . the specific things that tempted you? What were the things you were exposed to that planted that seed of desire? Let me give you a few ideas.

what is your pattern of temptation?

1 Common General Muscle Memory Triggers We Might Face Every Day

- Viewing movies with sexual humor or nudity
- Viewing TV programs with sexual innuendoes
- Browsing in a video store
- Reading personal ads
- Surfing the net
- Watching TV late at night
- Glancing through a Victoria's Secret catalogue
- Browsing through the magazines in a convenience store
- Driving by an adult bookstore
- Visiting a public rest stop

2 Common Muscle Memory Triggers We Might Face On Dates

- Being alone together
- Going to certain places during single dates
- Talking about sexual issues with girls
- Getting and giving massages
- Lying down together
- Kissing

I have found a few common triggers that I must avoid. I have developed some guidelines that help. Dannah and I have decided not to go to R-rated movies with the exception of an occasional historic-focused film. This is really hard for me because I love movies, particularly the intense action movies that are usually rated R. We check out the reviews before we head to a PG-13 movie because even those can be over the edge sexually. I have an Internet filter and wouldn't surf the net without it. And I try not to watch much TV, but when I do watch, I know what it is I want to see. No channel surfing. (OK, I break this one a lot, but I'm trying my best. Sometimes I think if God hadn't wanted us to surf He wouldn't have invented the remote control.) These guidelines and a few others help me avoid my triggers.

How Important Is Avoiding Triggers?

knowing your patterns is half the battle

Not only does stepping out of the current eliminate the planting of those desires, but it also helps you to avoid becoming chemically *addicted* to the sexual response created by superficial lures. Let's go back to those chemicals the brain creates when stimulated sexually. One of the chemicals released is called epinephrine. Here's the big catch: It runs through the bloodstream and returns to the brain to lock the vivid memory of that experience into your mind.[1] Your brain recalls a rush associated with that memory—it craves more like it.

The chemical release of sex is great, and when it is between a man and a wife, it

Same Things Keep Tangling You Up?

On September 27, 1958, the Army football team pulled a bit of pigskin over the eyes of their opponent, South Carolina. In the season-opening game, the Army offense lined up near the quarter back to hear the play call. Well, all but receiver Bill Carpenter lined up. He hunched some fifteen yards away. He did this for every play of the game, but it didn't seem to hinder his effectiveness. He was always in the right place at the right time. The media began to call him the "Lonely End." The Army team loved it and they continued using Carpenter in this fashion throughout the season. It drove the defense crazy. It was a great psychological tactic that helped result in an undefeated season for Army. At the end of the season, the coach revealed that though Carpenter could not hear the play, he watched the quarterback and was able to identify the play by the placement of his teammates feet, the way he rubbed his nose or tugged at his helmet.[2]

☆

is healthy and satisfying. When it is caused by sexual sin, it causes such a rush that we find ourselves running back for more. Each time we expose ourselves to the rush, it is like "shooting up" our mind. Dr. Mark Laaser, a nationally recognized specialist on sexual addictions, says, "Given the chemical changes it creates, sex fantasy addicts are, in reality, drug addicts."[3]

"Whoa!" you might be saying. "I'm no addict!"

I hope that is true. And I am guessing that for most of you, it is true. But now that you see how it works, do you really want to risk it by exposing yourself to the things that trigger your muscle memory? Every act of fantasy can cause an adrenaline rush that leads to another that leads to another that leads to another . . .

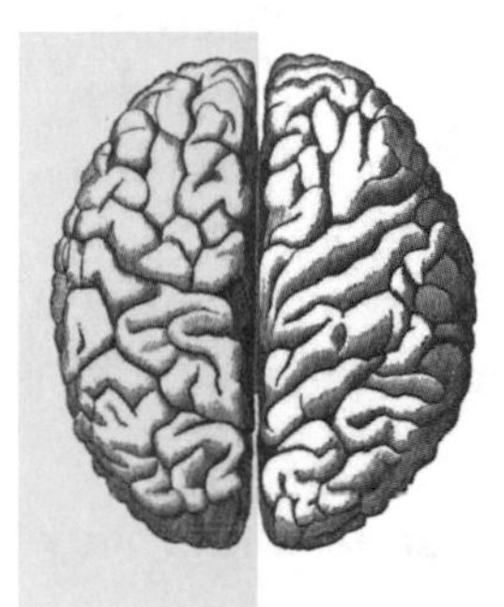

"In **any** battle between the **imagination** *and the* will, the **will** **loses** out every time."

BILLY GRAHAM

As quoted in Ed Murphy, The Handbook for Spiritual Warfare *(Nashville: Thomas Nelson, 1992), 122.*

Strengthen the right muscles.

Don't follow the mindless, empty-headed crowd as they saturate themselves with counterfeit pleasures. Expose yourself to fun Christian events, contemporary Christian music and TV and movies that depict healthy relationships. Choosing these will build up healthy appetites instead of insatiable hungers.

Sexual Integrity Challenge

Knowing our patterns and cycles is half the battle. You've identified the problem, now it's time to work it into your life. Use this area to write your muscle memory triggers on the left side. On the right side, you need to write a guideline that will help you eliminate the presence of that trigger in your life.

My Muscle Memory Triggers	How I Will Avoid Them

NOTES

1. American Family Association, "Pornography: A Report," Tupelo, Miss., 1989, 11.
2. Brad Herzog, "Whatever It Takes," *US Airways Attache,* October 2000, 60
3. Mark R. Laaser, *Faithful and True* (Grand Rapids: Zondervan, 1992), 26.

CHAPTER

11

Strategy #3:

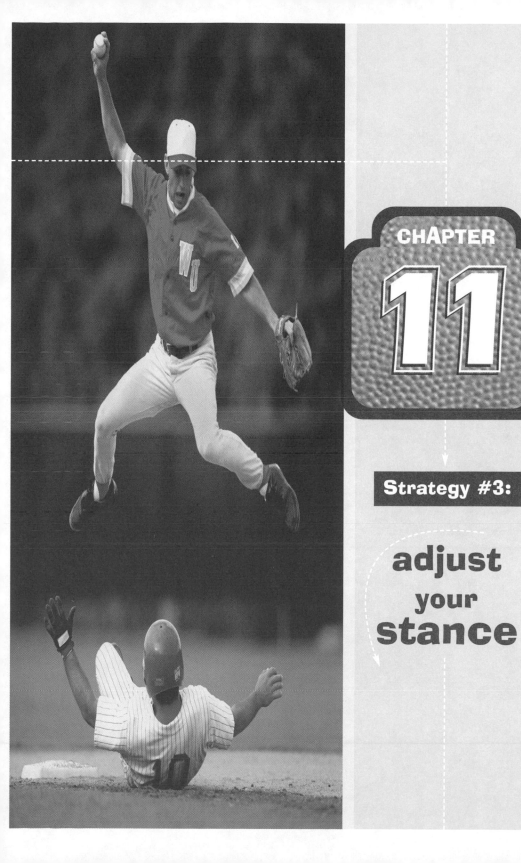

adjust your stance

It is obvious what kind of life develops out of trying to get your own way all the time: repetitive, loveless, cheap sex; a stinking accumulation of mental and emotional garbage; frenzied and joyless grabs for happiness; trinket gods; magic-show religion; paranoid loneliness; cutthroat competition; all-consuming-yet-never-satisfied wants; a brutal temper; an impotence to love or be loved; divided homes and divided lives; small-minded and lopsided pursuits, the vicious habit of depersonalizing everyone into a rival; uncontrolled and uncontrollable addictions; ugly parodies of community. I could go on . . . But what happens when we live God's way? He brings gifts into our lives, much the same way that fruit appears in an orchard—things like affection for others, exuberance about life, serenity. We develop a willingness to stick with things, a sense of compassion in the heart, and a conviction that a basic holiness permeates things and people. We find ourselves involved in loyal commitments, not needing to force our way in life, able to marshal and direct our energies wisely . . . Since this is the kind of life we have chosen, the life of the Spirit, let us make sure that we do not just hold it as an idea in our heads or a sentiment in our hearts, but work out its implications in every detail of our lives.

GALATIANS 5:19–23, 25 (*The Message*)

Strategy #3

adjust your stance

I pulled down the familiar street of Cedarville. It had been weeks since I'd seen my fiancée. I'd proposed to her just as I had always dreamed I would . . . in front of friends and family. I'd arranged for our engagement to be "written" into the Senior Night Play. The performance was the night before I graduated from Cedarville College in front of 2,000 friends and family. Dannah had been sitting in the audience expecting me to be back stage for the entire performance.

I came onto the stage with Kristen, a friend I'd lured into my dream scheme. We were talking about how many guys had been thrown into the lake recently. Everyone knew lake dunking was a Cedarville tradition for guys who became engaged.

"Speaking of engagement," said Kristen. "You and Dannah have been dating for a long time. When are you going to pop the question?"

That was all I needed. There was some carefully scripted dialogue while I searched for her in the audience, but the next thing I really remember was kneeling before her with a ring box open in my hand.

"Dannah Barker," I asked, "will you marry me?"

After a stunned pause, she managed to nod and whisper "yes." The audience roared with excitement! It was quite a night.

Immediately, we were to be separated for six months as she stayed at Cedarville to complete her degree. It stunk to be apart, and the phone bills were high.

Now as I neared the gravel driveway beside the big, old house where Dannah was spending the summer, I pulled in—and there she was. She looked good . . . boy, did she look good.

In moments we were in each others arms. She smelled good. She felt good. I gave her the kind of hug that said "romance" to her and "what a body" to me.

Suddenly we were in the living room kissing passionately. This was unfamiliar territory. It was against every unspoken boundary we'd established. Where had the seconds gone? I don't think we'd even spoken a single word to each other. We crashed onto the sofa together.

"Whoa!" I said standing up almost as quickly as we hit the fabric. "I think I better leave."

In Dannah's eyes I saw her feelings: rejection. She did not understand what was going on with my body.

Although my body said, "Go for it" my boundaries said "No."

"Why don't you come with me?" I suggested to spare her feelings. "We'll go to Deb Haffey's house."

Deb was my college professor, my mentor and my friend. She and her husband had agreed to put me up for the weekend. I was now hoping that Dannah and I could hang out at her house during the day. It certainly wouldn't have been my first choice to be under the watchful eye of an older, wiser person, but I was certain it was necessary to protect my bride-to-be.

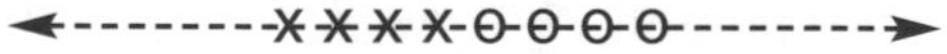

Being truly alone with my fiancée for the first time brought a whole new level of temptation that I did not expect. The commitment had been made. Soon I could fully know her intimately. And we were eight hours away from family—and accountability—in the middle of a little town that was nearly empty. Talk about immediate enticement! I hadn't been in this place of temptation before, but I knew I had to get out quickly or I would regret my actions. I chose, mostly because I loved Dannah and I had predetermined boundaries, to not act out the desire in every inch of my body.

talk about immediate enticement!

When we let our desires become sins—whether looking at pornography or having sex with someone we are dating—that's called acting out. *Acting out is sexual sin in action.* We've allowed our desires to be acted out in the flesh. James 1:15 says, "After desire has conceived, it gives birth to sin." In other words—just like a woman who is pregnant fully expects to give birth—once the sexual desire is in there, it is imminent that it will be making its way out. It grows and builds, and one day it is a fully birthed sin in the form of destructive sexual behavior of some kind.

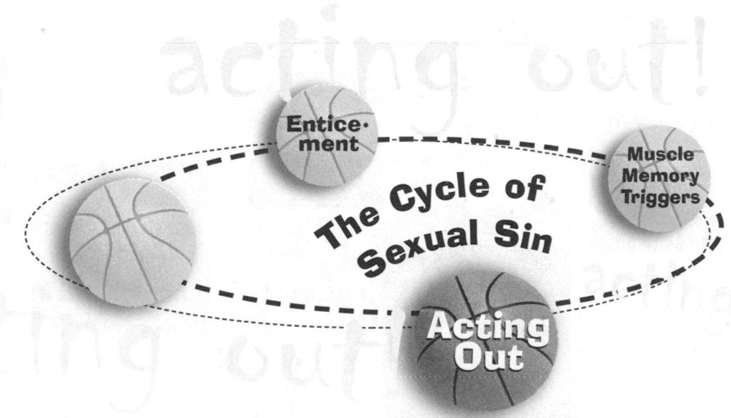

Dealing with lust when there's not a girl involved is one thing. We might act out through masturbation, using pornography, or fantasizing even when a girl isn't with us. Each has its consequences. But dealing with the

temptation to not become sexual with a girl is an entirely different kind of temptation. You have to consider your boundaries when you're dating.

stay in bounds!

I believe a man can evaluate his sexual perversion or his sexual strength within dating relationships by taking the test God gave us in the letter to the Galatian people in chapter five. You've probably seen the tests that you take in magazines or on TV to see if you are a trivia buff or a person with a good vocabulary. Well, the apostle Paul offers two checklists to help determine which approach describes us most clearly. If we are honest, we probably have **some numbers to circle** under each list, but the one that rules our lives is the one that flavors our relationships. Which are you? A Relationship Rookie or an **NFL** AllStar (**N**ever **F**ailing **L**ove, that is)? Circle one or the other by each number.

Relationship Rookie

1 **You don't stick around for relationships to get meaningful** *("an impotence to love or to be loved").*

2 **You're sure the next girl or fantasy will make you happy** *("frenzied and joyless grabs for happiness").*

3 **You don't focus on the big picture of your life** *("small-minded and lopsided pursuits").*

4 **You have memories, guilt, and shame from past relationships** *("accumulation of mental and emotional garbage and divided lives").*

5 **The decisions you make in dating are for you!** *("trying to get your own way all the time").*

6 **Repetitive sexual encounters or fantasies that make you feel cheap** *("repetitive, loveless, cheap sex").*

7 **You date a girl even at the expense of a friendship with a buddy.**

8 **Your relationship with God is about what you can get from Him** *("magic-show religion").*

9 **Your relationships and pastimes break boundaries and are never satisfying** *("all-consuming wants" and "uncontrollable addictions").*

NFL AllStar

1 **You genuinely like other people** *("affection for others").*

2 **You are enthusiastic about what the days will bring, but not anxious** *("exuberance about life").*

3 **You focus on God and get time alone with Him each day** *("serenity").*

4 **Your past relationships have ended in healthy friendships** *("a willingness to stick with things").*

5 **You consider a girl's feelings before you do anything** *("a sense of compassion in the heart").*

6 **You strive for purity and believe those around you to be doing the same** *("a conviction that a basic holiness permeates things and people").*

7 **You stick with friendships through thick and thin. A girl would not come between you and a buddy** *("loyal commitments").*

8 **You kindly accept things that don't go your way as God's plan** *("not needing to force our way in life").*

9 **You are spending your time on worthwhile relationships and have healthy boundaries** *("able to marshal and direct our energies wisely").*

So, are you a Relationship Rookie or an NFL AllStar? Before marriage, I had a lot of friends who were girls. When Dannah and I began to date, she thought it curious that most of the girls I had dated in the past were still my friends. We had lunch together if we ran into each other in the cafeteria. We sat near each other if we had a class together. We had a healthy friendship that followed our generally short period of dating. That's because our dating relationships were governed by a genuine affection. I was concerned with how I treated that girl because I knew it could have a long-term impact. I considered the future before I did anything. I accepted it kindly (if somewhat dejectedly) when a relationship didn't go where I had hoped it would. And my buddies were who I spent the core of my time with. I didn't come by that naturally. I learned the hard way.

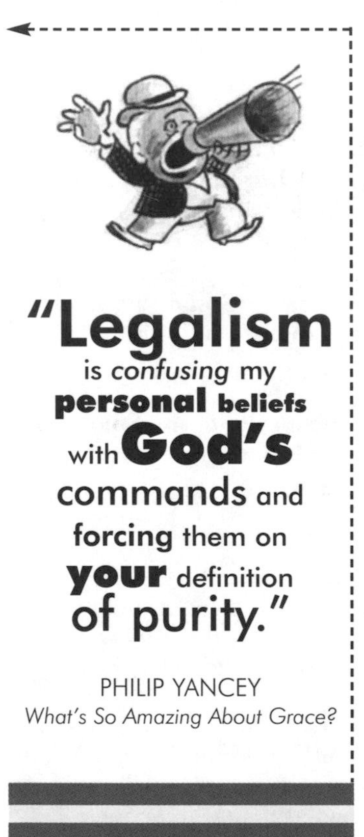

"Legalism is confusing my personal beliefs with God's commands and forcing them on your definition of purity."
PHILIP YANCEY
What's So Amazing About Grace?

In my first major dating relationship, I was a major loser, even though I never actually had sex with the girl. I acted selfishly in how I treated her. I never considered the big picture of her life or mine when we were together. I was only concerned with my own desires. Have fun. Feel good. Be popular. The relationship ended very badly. I have deep regrets about it. I am sorry for how I treated her and for the direction I took the relationship.

So, how do you avoid that? After all, it comes quite naturally to most of us. We've got to establish some guidelines that create a genuine desire to be an NFL AllStar.

Am I suggesting that we have a list of rules to follow? Yes, actually, I am. I have a list that I follow and you should have one too. Is that legalism? No. Legalism is, as author Philip Yancey says, forcing your own personal preferences on others and acting like they are biblical commandments.

Paul speaks harshly against legalism in Colossians 2:20–23 when he says, "Since you died with Christ to the basic principles of this world, why, as though you still belonged to it, do you submit to its rules: 'Do not handle! Do not taste! Do not touch!?' These are all destined to perish with use, because they are based on human commands and teachings. Such regulations indeed have an appearance of wisdom . . . but they lack any value in restraining sensual indulgence." Paul says that conforming to rules fails to fix the problem and denies you the opportunity to develop the maturity needed to live life with integrity.

Legalism . . . no! Strong heart-motivated guidelines for your life . . . yes! If you have them, you will be molded into what God desires for you to be. Great men do not occur spontaneously. They are molded and created from an inner desire for greatness. They are produced only after submitting themselves to a disciplined lifestyle. It's a lifestyle that at its base always struggles to be distinctive and to create a legacy that lives longer than the life that brought it into being.

Are you ready to submit yourself to the disciplined lifestyle? I have a few questions for you. They will help you develop a list of heart-motivated boundaries.

what happens when we live God's way?

Who will you date?

Who you choose to date says a lot about whether you truly want to be governed by a disciplined lifestyle. A mother of a teenaged boy I know brought home his girlfriend one afternoon. She came in with a mod short haircut. Her T-shirt was even shorter. Her exposed belly bore a trendy belly-button ring.

After some small talk, the mother asked the girl, "Why do you wear that belly ring?"

The Christian young woman responded, "Because it's sexy!"

I don't know about your mom, but mine would have blown a gasket if I brought home a girl like that.

Do you know who you will date, or do you regularly play the game of "Duck, Duck, Date," in which your strategy is to either date anything that walks by or date as many as you possibly can? Both are not such good ideas.

Rebecca St. James on **What a Girl Is Looking For**

Rebecca St. James is a popular singer and songwriter. She also is single and has a specific kind of guy in mind when it comes to what a Christian girl is looking for.

"I definitely have a vision of a little bit of what he will be like. I . . . kind of picture him just having this consuming love for God that is just so beautiful and so challenging to me. That leads me and challenges me. I definitely want him to be a spiritual leader to me. I think that because I know that he is going to be a man after God's own heart and purity is going to be important to him too. He is going to be waiting for me. That helps comfort me in the waiting process."[1]

A friend of mine liked the "Duck, Duck, Date" game because he wanted to date as many girls as he could. He was handsome, funny, and a leader in his Christian world. He led the girls he dated to the Lord a lot of the time. But he also had desires that needed to be kept in check. He took a risk and grabbed up a pretty wild girl just for fun one time. She was not the kind of girl he would have chosen to marry. He got her pregnant. After prayerful examination and many tears, they decided to marry. Yikes! That's not the kind of proposal I would have liked to have made.

Dating is not a game. You can define it as going out on Friday nights in a car alone or as having a relationship that is monitored by either family or friends. Either way, its purpose is to search for the person with whom you will have the most significant relationship of your life. Dating can also help you to learn about yourself and the kind of wife you hope to have someday. That's pretty serious business.

Do you know what you are looking for in a girl? Or do you just date on a whim?

Take this chance to write down a few qualities you'd like in the girl you marry.

The One

What does she like? What does she look like? Who does she love more than you? (You'd better be able to answer that question!) Even before I knew Dannah, I knew what I wanted in a girl. In my younger years, I dreamed of being president, so I wanted a girl who could speak well and handle the pressures of a busy lifestyle. My dream career changed, but my dream girl never did. I wanted a girl who was beautiful inside and out and whose walk with God amazed me. I hoped she would sing. Dannah doesn't . . . at least, not outside of the shower. Some things just aren't that important. Take some time and dream of "the one" right now.

Look up 2 Corinthians 6:14. Is there anything you need to add to your list after considering this?

Where will you date?

This question has to be answered by you and only you. It's gotten somewhat complicated these days, as you might have noticed. Joshua Harris' *I Kissed Dating Goodbye* opened the floodgates. Now the bookshelves are filled with titles like *The Dating Trap, I Gave Dating A Chance,* and *Boundaries in Dating*. The book in your hands is not about dating. It's about sexual integrity. But we definitely have to consider the subject for a brief moment. You have some options.

Will you date under the watchful eyes of your parents? Some call this courting. I have a single adult friend who was living like a Relationship Rookie and everyone knew it. His sexual escapades were office fodder the next day. Then he met the Savior and was a new man. I have seen few people change like he did. He made the decision to stop dating. He waited to see if the Lord would bring someone into his life where a healthy friendship developed into something more. God did just that, but my friend wisely did not trust himself to take her out. He asked her parents to supervise their courtship because he knew his weakness.

> "God's most powerful weapon, **grace**, has been *cast aside* in our efforts to be **spiritually pure**. The modern-day Pharisee ***who focuses on*** **avoiding** *sin* is **still** focused on sin. *In fact, he is little different* from the person who is **consumed** by sin. Both are obsessed with sin—one to **avoid it**, the *other* to **live** in it."
>
> TED ROBERTS
> *Pure Desire*

His first moment of physical touch with his wife was at the marriage altar. I believe him to be a great man of God because of this choice. But his choice was not made out of the current wave of popularity for courtship. This was eight years ago. His choice was made out of the motivation of his heart to be great for God.

Dannah and I see a lot of young people choosing courtship out of a heart motivated by God. We also see a lot of young people doing it because it is the popular thing to do. Dannah interviewed Joshua Harris for her book. He said himself that courting has to be from the motivation of your heart. Do you think that perhaps God would call you to choose courting?

You can choose to date as in "going out" together, but then you have to ask yourself . . . where will we go? Dannah and I dated and had a great time. One day climbing through the springs and rocks of Yellow Springs, Ohio, I snapped a couple of rolls of film taking pictures of her. Another time we splurged on a $100 meal high above the city of Columbus. I remember surprising her one day with tickets to the Ice Capades followed by a tour of the Dayton Art Museum. (Oh, the things you do when you are in love. This was *not* my idea of an exciting day.) We played laser tag together and visited the shore together with our families. The standard for us was to avoid, as much as possible, being truly alone.

You can have the privacy and feeling of being alone without putting yourself in a place where things can become physical. We went to the library a lot or we did our laundry together. We went skiing or shopping. We were in places where we had our own space but people were nearby.

Do you feel OK with dating? Where will you date so that it's a fun positive experience free of temptation?

What physical boundaries will you have on your dates?

That's the big question. So big I've saved a whole chapter for it. Read on, because this is the part that truly separates the Relationship Rookie from the NFL AllStar. There's no doubt that you will face the opportunity to hit a "home run" at some point. The truth is, striking out may be your best option!

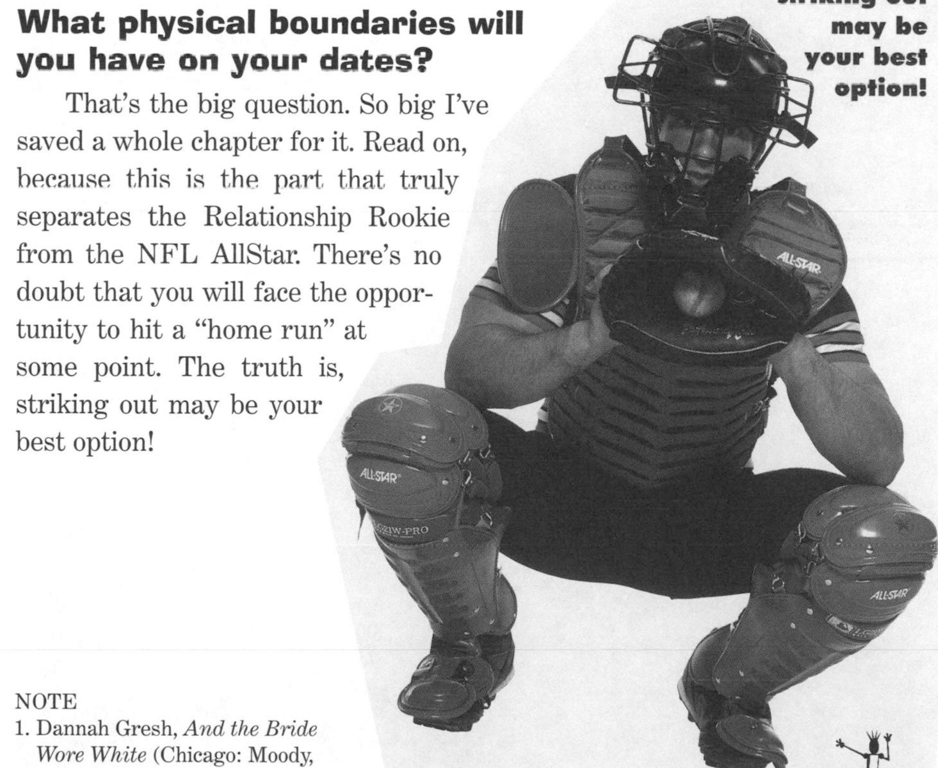

NOTE
1. Dannah Gresh, *And the Bride Wore White* (Chicago: Moody, 1999), 166.

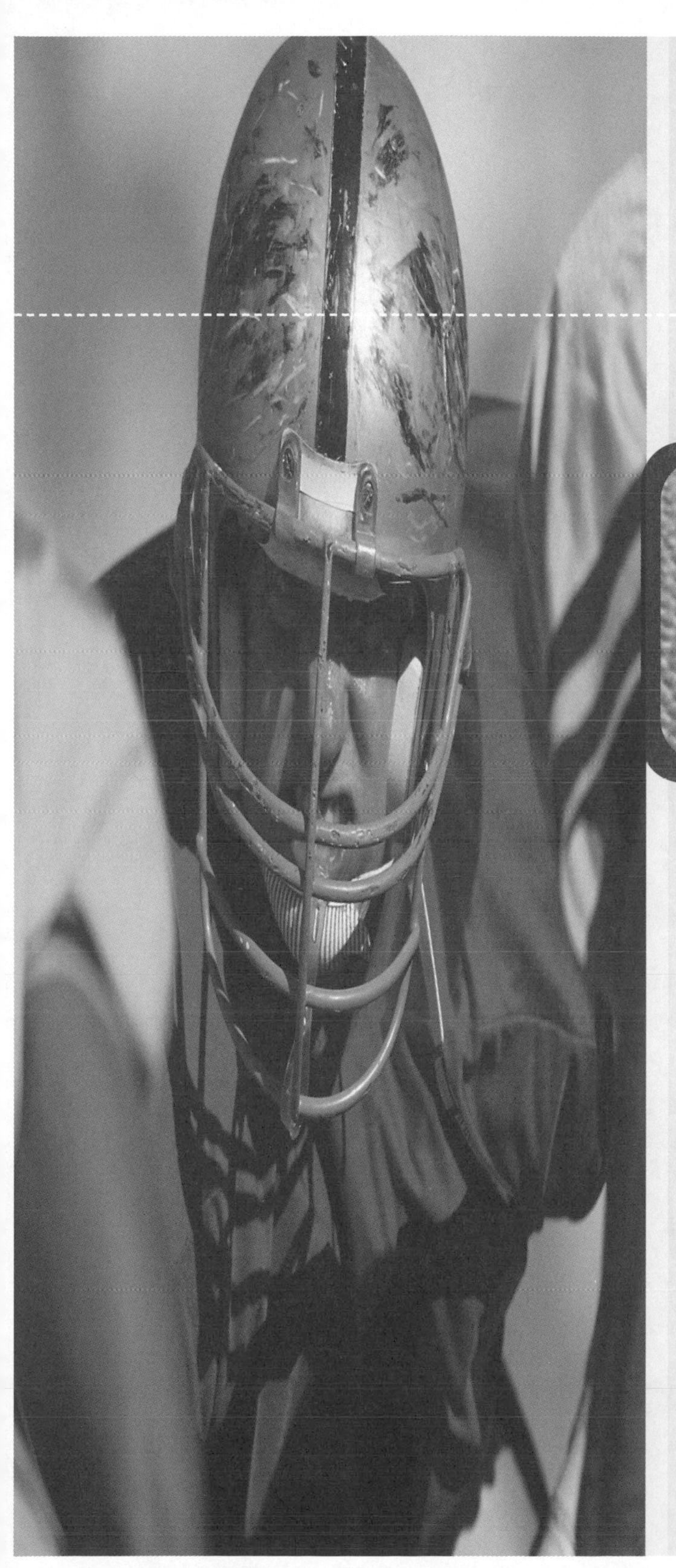

CHAPTER 12

Strategy #4:

Guard your future . . . and Hers

Train yourself to be godly.

1 TIMOTHY 4:7

Strategy #4

Guard your future . . . and Hers

Man, are women different from men! You may have noticed this living with your mom or your sisters. For example, did you know that the average girl speaks 25,000 words a day as opposed to a guy's 10,000 words? That's an accident waiting to happen if you ask me!

Let me prepare you for a few things early on. Don't bang your head against the wall for years to fix problems that can't be fixed. There are certain things you'll have to live with when you are married.

1. You will *not* be able to use towels hanging in your own bathroom. They're for decoration only.

2. Your wife will want the bed made in the morning even though you're going to be sleeping in it again that night.

3. If your wife uses the smoke detector as the oven timer and your dinner looks and tastes like a piece of charcoal, *do not . . . I repeat, do not . . .* make a negative comment. The dinner table is no place for constructive criticism.

God knew we were different. The Hebrew word for man is actually "hard." The Hebrew word for woman is "soft." We are as different from females as hard is from soft.

Sexually we are very different. Here's a quiz. What's the primary sex organ of the man? Got a guess. OK, take it up a few feet . . . there you go - the brain! The brain is the primary sex organ of the guy. Try to get aroused without it. It's all about what we see and how the brain responds.

What's the primary sex organ of the woman? This will surprise some of you. The heart is the primary sex organ of the woman. Unless her heart is warmed up to you, she probably will not be interested in you physically. It takes time, romance, and tenderness to arouse a woman.

Think of her future.

Focus with me for a minute.

It stands to reason that if a girl's heart is closely connected to her sexuality, it can easily be broken by sexuality. You and I cannot even grasp the depth of that.

When we were dating, Dannah was a beautiful example of purity. I never thought for even a second that she could have struggled with sexual temptation. I never asked. I just assumed that she had made it. She didn't make it. In one relationship, things got out of control. She tried to tell me many times before we were engaged. Then, she tried again after we were engaged . . . and many times after we were married. It was too painful for her and she couldn't speak the words she dreaded.

Five years after we were married, the hidden grief became too much for her. One night in our bedroom she struggled through a confession. After ten years, I saw pain in her face that I cannot even describe. You'd think that in ten years she would have achieved some level of healing. She had not. How I wish you could have seen the look on her face. You would never even consider taking a girl's virginity from her.

Dannah gets letters from girls every day whose lives have been ripped apart by some guy's selfish sexual quest. These guys are not monsters. They're guys like me and maybe like you. I hope in reading some of these letters you can get some sense of how damaged the girls become. I want to emphasize that these letters are from Christian girls and that they are not uncommon. I wish they were. This girl wrote to Dannah to tell her about having had sex with a guy who has dumped her.

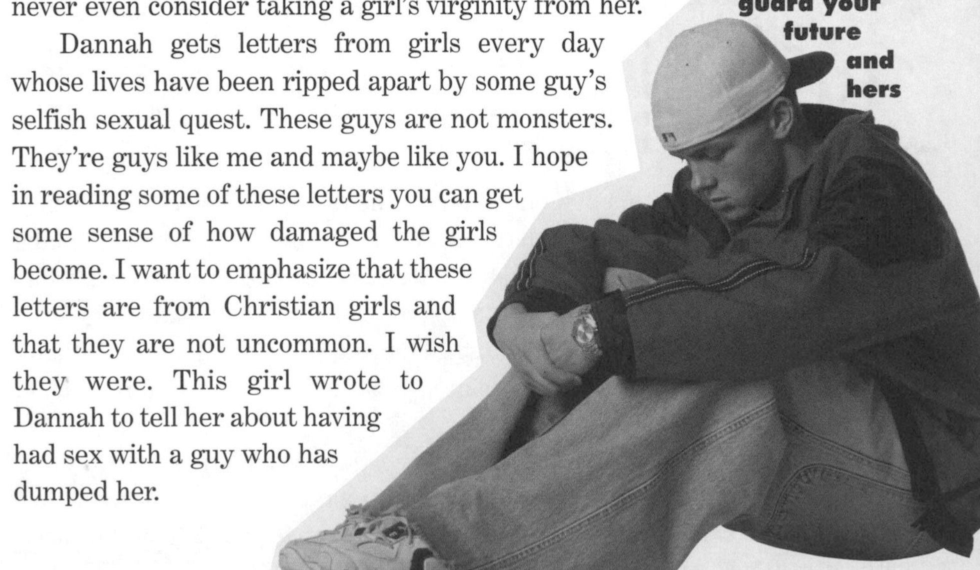
guard your future and hers

"I'm destroyed on the inside but a good actress on the outside that everybody sees. At least once a week I don't get out of bed and go to school. I'm so destroyed inside and can't take this anymore.

Just today my mom made a joke out of me having a breakdown and I started bawling my eyes out 'cause it's true. I feel like that's what's gonna happen. This pain is so overwhelming and this guy doesn't even care. How do I get through this?"

Another girl wrote to talk about the long process of recovery she went through after having sex with multiple partners—something that's far too common these days and very dangerous, given AIDS and other sexually transmitted diseases.

"I confessed to my sister what had happened to me, and she made sure I got the help I needed. I sought therapy from a Christian counselor, and was soon diagnosed with clinical depression, and put on an antidepressant.

In my head this wasn't enough. I was no longer a person in my head. I was numb, devoid of any emotion, so I tried to kill myself. I took pills and cut at my wrists, but God wasn't through with me, and refused to let me go."

She ended up really getting on track with God. It's too bad that selfish sexual acts caused so much turmoil in her life.

Many other girls approach Dannah when she speaks. One was a senior at a Christian college. She came to Dannah trembling with tears. Her story went something like this:

"I always knew I wanted to be a missionary and I really loved God. When I was old enough, I committed myself to courting rather than dating. My mother courted. My grandmother courted. That's just what we do. I thought that courting was safe, but I found out that it wasn't.

At the age of fifteen, I gave away the gift that belonged to my husband during a foolish moment of passion. I soon broke that relationship off and never courted again . . . until recently. The only reason I agreed to court this guy was because if I didn't I would have to tell my dad about my sin. I didn't want to do that. After several months of courting we fell in love. He wants to be a missionary, too. He's perfect for me in every way. He proposed to me through my father two weeks ago and it's the most agonizing thing I've ever done, but I said "no." He figured out why and says he still loves me and wants to marry me. I just don't think I deserve to be loved like that."

Imagine being so emotionally hurt by something that you punish yourself forever. That's what this girl was willing to do. She and Dannah had a long talk and she went on to accept that the tremendous healing of God . . . *and* that proposal.

To take a girl's virginity is to take a part of her. The suicide rate among sexually active teenage girls is six times that of the suicide rate among their virgin peers.[1] Get this! **You cannot take a girl's virginity without creating emotional scars in her that may last for years or perhaps a lifetime if she doesn't find God's healing and hope.** For one brief moment, stop thinking with your sex drive and think of her future.

You would be proud of the future you can give her—whether you end up with her or not—if you just control yourself.

Read this!

"Dear Dannah, Do you remember me? I was an engaged girl who was being so tempted . . . and you were a great encouragement to me. Well, I have been married now for 18 days and I am having the time of my life! We waited with the grace of our Lord (and Him alone through us!!!) until our wedding night and we had a **great** *honeymoon. I am married and sharing such a special thing with my very best friend!"*

When you are with a girl, take just one second to think of the future you can give her.

Think of YOUR future.

So many guys have such a double standard. It's OK for them to have sex with girls, but they want their wives to have waited for them. As Josh McDowell once said, "Most guys don't like used furniture but they love to be in the antiquing business."[2] These same guys don't stop to think of the fact that sex will be more fun if they wait!

I want sex to be a fantastic experience for you, too. I want you to know the fantastic, unashamed blessing of God's gift of sex on your wedding night. For it to be that huge, you have to protect it. Otherwise, you lose so much of the newness and excitement. (I don't even have to mention the risks such as sexually transmitted diseases and possible pregnancy, do I?)

predetermine where to stop How do you protect your future and hers? You predetermine where you will stop.

Remember how the body's autonomic nervous system responds? It automatically creates arousal. Just as it responds to new stimuli, it can become less responsive to old sensations. For example, the first time you hold hands with a girl you can get a rush out of it. It feels pretty good, and it satisfies some level of your desire for closeness. But eventually, that wears off and you find yourself wanting the same satisfaction. You find it maybe in hugs or a tender kiss. Eventually, that wears off and you want to move to the next level. At some point, you really stop thinking—at least with your intellect—and the autonomic nervous system takes control. You pass the point of no return.

Dannah interviewed Steven Curtis Chapman for her book. She asked him a question which he answered very boldly.

> **Dannah:** You have lived a godly example for so many people, but no matter who you are, there will always be temptation. You have made choices to live a lifestyle of purity. What would be one moment that you could say, "I chose a path of purity in my life and I am proud of that?"
>
> **SCC:** Well, our life is made up of a lot of those moments. Hmmm? I am hesitant only because I think, "How honest do I want to be?" There was a relationship that I was in long ago. I was out on my own, all alone for the first time. There was a girl that I was dating. It was not a really deep relationship. We were kissing and had kind of gotten involved. But I had always known that I was saving myself. I wanted my wedding night to be the first night I was intimate and it would be with the woman I married. But I knew that in this relationship if I wanted to go down that route, she was willing. It was like a bucket of water in my face. It was not even an option. I cannot say it is a moment that I was proud of, as much as it was a moment that God had really trained me for. For a brief moment, I was caught up in the motion. I was a nineteen-year-old young man and a light came on and I said, "Think about all the implications, physically, emotionally, spiritually." That was the beginning of the end of that relationship. God had built a real strong foundation in me. I am thankful that sex is and was an amazing thing on my wedding night because I saved myself for that night. I am so thankful for people along the way to help me build that foundation." [3]

Did you hear that? He was trained for *that* moment. (His memory muscle kicked in just like it was supposed to!) Just like 1 Timothy 4:7 says, you've got to train yourself to be godly. Steven Curtis Chapman had considered where he would draw the line, and taking the time to do that was what got him out of that situation.

I think Joseph trained for that moment too. Think about it. Potiphar's wife was one of the richest and most popular women in Egypt. She was the celebrity of the day. She was hot! She'd probably teased him many times. But he'd trained himself for the moment. And so he made that fast, strategic exit! He knew when to run.

Have you taken time to consider where you will draw the line physically? It's time to do that right now.

Sexual Integrity Challenge

If you are truly thinking about her future and yours, you should never find yourself in a truly compromising situation. Unfortunately, I know some of you will find yourselves in that position. Are you prepared to stop things? Let's look at the "Steps to Sexual Activity" together and prepare *yourself* for that moment.

First, draw a firm black line showing where you will stop physical contact. Predetermining where you will stop things will help you when temptation arises. It will set off a mental alarm for you. Please consider that you and I were created to have high sexual drives. It doesn't take much to quickly slide down that slope into full sexual activity. Be extremely conservative when you draw that black line.

Next, consider through prayer whether God would be pleased to see you doing the particular physical activities you're permitting below that firm black line. If you have any doubt at all, go back to the chart and move that line by one step. Remember that God's standard is that there not be a "hint" of sexual immorality within your life.

Third, let me suggest that you draw a line at a higher level for physical activity before you are engaged. For example, let's say you drew your firm black line above number five. You have determined that your firm black line will remind you to stop as soon as soft kissing begins to turn into something more. It can be really hard after you are engaged to stick to your standard. Very hard. Your body and your mind are telling you that you've almost made it and temptation can really blindside you.

But you have almost made it. Don't blow it.

1 Looking at a girl and making eye contact

(Remember we are visually stimulated.)

2 Talking with a girl

(Hey, ever notice how much passion talk can create?)

3 Holding hands

(This can be a nice sign of attachment.)

4 Hands on shoulders and hands on waist

(Can you handle this? Can she?)

5 Kissing on the cheek or softly kissing on the lips

(This is a sweet, innocent kiss.)

6 Open-mouthed passionate kissing

(A new desire awakens.)

7 Petting while clothed

8 Experimental nakedness

9 Oral sex

10 Sexual Intercourse

NOTES

1. Barth D. Kirby and Fetro Leland, "Reducing the Risk: Impact of a New Curriculum Among Youths In California". *Family Plan Perspectives (*1991) 23:253–63.
2. Josh McDowell and Paul Lewis, *Givers, Takers and Other Kinds of Lovers* (Wheaton, Ill.: Tyndale, 1980), 33.
3. Dannah Gresh, *And the Bride Wore White* (Chicago: Moody, 2000), 163.

CHAPTER 13

Strategy #5a:

receive the Father's Love

"You're blessed when you're at the end of your rope. With less of you there is more of God and His rule. You're blessed when you feel you've lost what is most dear to you. Only then can you be embraced by the One most dear to you."

MATTHEW 5:3–4 *(The Message)*

Strategy #5a

receive the Father's Love

"Close your eyes," said Tippy Duncan.

Tippy was one of my dearest friends. Though in her fifties, her eyes twinkled with childlike joy. She was energy in human form. I had a hard time keeping up with her on our weekly walks. She had lovingly added me to the long list of souls she mentored. Through her wise counsel, I was finally . . . at the ripe age of twenty-eight . . . in the process of redirecting my energies to Christ. That wasn't always an easy task.

We had stopped walking. We sat down on her back porch.

"Close my eyes?" I mumbled. I shifted back and forth. "I hate these kind of exercises."

"Do you want to feel better, Bob?" she asked. She didn't scold. She didn't condescend. She just said it. That's how Tippy was. I never felt like she was angry with me when I talked to her about my weaknesses; she just seemed sad for me. She made me feel safe.

She smiled and her eyes invited me to cooperate with her plan.

"Oh, OK," I said as I reluctantly closed my eyes.

"Think back to the vilest thing you have ever done." She said matter-of-factly and then paused to let me think.

"I want you to picture yourself there at that moment as if it were happening right now," she explained. "Think about how you feel. See what you are doing. Note the environment around you."

I felt a shroud of darkness hover over me as I returned to that place.

It was my weakest moment. There wasn't a shred of sexual integrity in me then as I saw myself there. I felt sick to my stomach.

"Now, I want you to watch as Jesus enters the scene and sees you there," Tippy said calmly.

I didn't like where this was heading.

"What does Jesus do?" Tippy asked.

I couldn't even face it. The shame overwhelmed me. After what seemed like an eternity of silence, Tippy answered the question for me. "Jesus embraces you, Bob." she said.

Right in my own mind, Jesus' glance caught mine, and in His eyes I saw the same look Tippy always gave me. He was not mad. He was not disappointed. He was just simply sad for me.

My face began to tense as I fought off emotion. Wetness filled the corners of my eyes. I squeezed them tight to stop the flow. My body tensed, but before I could race away from the emotion, Tippy pushed me further.

My mind played the picture. Jesus walked close to me. He touched me. There in my filth and shame, He actually reached out and touched me. He embraced me and held me; then He quietly led me away from that place.

Could it be that this Savior of mine had seen my deepest sin and still came close to touch me? Could it be that His love was greater than my filth and shame?

←-------XXXX-OOOO-------→

Memories. They can be more convicting than any judge or jury. If my friend, Tippy, were asking you to close your eyes and picture the vilest thing you'd ever done, what would it be? How would that make you feel? Unless you've already allowed God to deal with that sin, the feeling can be nauseating. That's shame.

Shame is the last stage of sexual sin. It's the feeling

shame is like having the skin of your soul ripped off

we get hours after we act out in some way. Maybe it was just a fantasy, or perhaps you actually looked at pornography on the Internet. Or maybe things got out of control with a girl. Maybe you flipped through a porn magazine, visited an adult bookstore, or experimented with homosexuality. You found yourself with the same lonely, desperate feeling you had the last time you acted out. This is shame.

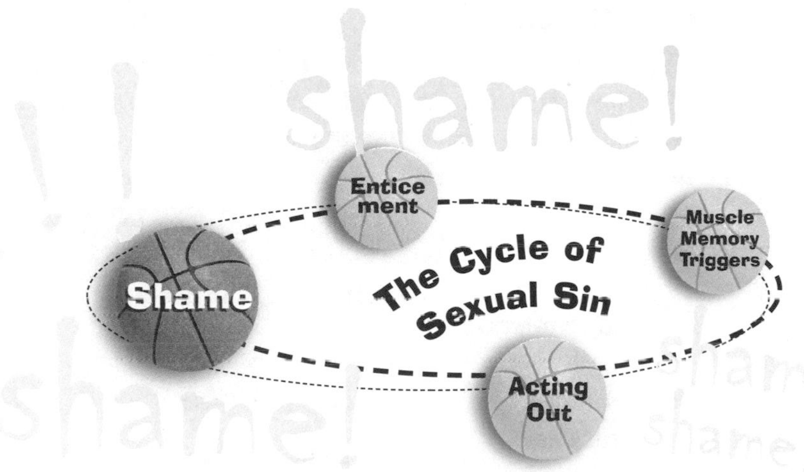

Guilt Versus Shame

Shame is not the same as guilt. Guilt can actually benefit us. Guilt is God's tool to address specific sinful behaviors. It tells us we need to redirect our habits and choices. Guilt says, "I should not have done that. *That* was bad." Guilt is like the skin of your soul. It protects your mind and emotions. If your skin touched something that could burn you, it would send pulses to your brain that would help you get out of danger. That's how guilt works.

guilt is like the skin of your soul

Shame is a tool of Satan, which distorts guilt. Shame says, "*I* am bad." It is a terribly painful feeling that never ceases. It drives us into a lonelier place where we cannot find accountability or guidance to heal. Shame is like having the skin of your soul ripped off, actually taking with it the emotions that lie beneath. Psychologist John Bradshaw wrote, "Toxic shame . . . is no longer an emotion that signals our limits, it is a state of being, a core identity. Toxic shame gives you a sense of worthlessness."[1]

These feelings and thoughts come from Satan. It's in his job description to accuse you.[2] Shame is his scheme to get you to pull away from God in a vain attempt to "get your act together." You find yourself also pulling away from others and the hope to heal. In the separation, we further rip away at any kind of intimacy. Yet we still crave that intimacy. So we look for false intimacy through sexual stimulation, which only leads to more shame.

Intimacy Versus Shame

Shame is actually the opposite of what God had in mind when He created sex. Shame takes us as far away from a truthful sexual experience as you can possibly go, because shame is the opposite of intimacy.

Intimacy is that quiet place of vulnerability where you feel completely safe and no longer alone. Adam and Eve knew this intimacy in Genesis 2:25. That verse says that "the man and his wife were both naked, and they felt no shame." The physical nakedness portrayed a deep spiritual and emotional openness. It wasn't about the nakedness. The fact was, the nakedness had little to do with it. They were comfortable with their nakedness because emotionally and spiritually they felt comfortable, honest, free to be emotional with each other and ready to be vulnerable. That's intimacy.

Intimacy	**Shame**
Comfortable	**Self-conscious**
Honest	**Denial**
Emotional	**Numb**
Vulnerable	**Control-oriented**

Guys have a hard time being comfortable with intimacy. Yet, we crave it at the very base of our souls and are not satisfied until we find it. Why? Because until we find it we feel lonely. We cycle viciously in our search for intimacy. We hunger for a truthful, pure intimate relationship with a woman and find ourselves in a period of seeking for that at any cost. Then, because we become afraid or impatient or because it is hard work, our lust goes into overdrive as it sees the illusion of intimacy in pornography, masturbation, and loveless sex. Since acting out like that creates shame, we find ourselves so far away from *intimacy* that we feel even more lonely. The cycle continues.

For a number of years in junior and senior high, the great sexual temptation I faced made me feel guilty. Somewhere along the way the guilt became shame. I pulled away from friends, from family, from God. I allowed the shame to rule my life.

Many times I was at the end of my rope, as they say. I was either a junior or senior in college when I wrote this:

JUNE 31

What frustration! The summer is going worse than I ever thought was possible. For the first time God is scaring me. Pulling out all the security and success that I have built up. Taking me down to zero and beyond . . . A positive attitude is hard to convey when you're feeling pretty negative yourself.

I guess I thought that God was punishing me and that when I straightened it out God would bless me again. There must be more to it than that. Security has to rest in Jesus, not in my abilities . . . The very last thread, the very end of the rope must be given to the Lord and then He'll let you hang on.

Many times I returned to that place of frustration because of my shame. I just couldn't quite let go of the rope. I didn't know that God's love was ready to welcome me back and sustain me day by day.

The Prodigal Son: A Relationship Rookie?

The Bible doesn't really say that he was sexually crazed, but the prodigal son described in Luke 15 definitely would score points in our test for being a Relationship Rookie. (Remember that from chapter 11?) He clearly tried to get his way all of the time. His relationship with his dad was about what he could get out of it. He was competitive to the max with his brother. He had small-minded and lopsided pursuits . . . crazy parties night after night to the point of not being able to keep a decent job. He was incapable of loving or accepting love. It's not a stretch for me to believe that he had his share of repetitive, loveless sex while roaming the earth with his wealth. No doubt, he found a way to feed his uncontrollable addictions.

And I bet everyone back home caught wind of his shameless escapades from time to time.

Then, he bottomed out. He finds himself at the end of his rope, as we always do when we live like that. His wealth is gone. His friends have seen him for what he is and they are gone, too. He has no way to feed his addictions or his small-minded pursuits. He finds himself sitting in a pigpen eating slop. He starts thinking of ways he can "fix" things himself. He really has no other option than to return home, but feels obligated to offer a solution. Filled with shame, he rehearses his lines and plans a formal, non-intimate proposal for his father.[3]

could God possibly welcome me back?

He was right where I have been many times. Have you been there? Wondering how God could possibly welcome you back, even as a bench warmer on His team?

That's how the prodigal comes to his father. He comes empty-handed. He lets go of the rope—made up of pride, self-will, and shame—and reaches out for his father. It's his last resort. He shows up smelling like a pigpen—encrusted in pig slop and waste.

His father runs toward the stench. He embraces his son. He kisses his filthy son and leads him home. There he wraps him in robes of honor.

That's a father's love for you. That is how God loves you.

I'd like to ask you the question Tippy once asked me. First, imagine yourself in the vilest place you've ever been. Think about how you feel. See what you are doing. Note the environment around you. Now, watch as Jesus enters the scene.

What does Jesus do?

Let me answer for you. He embraces you.

How can He? How can He reach past the shame? How can He see my sin and still embrace me time after time after time? Grace! It's all about the grace

of a loving Father that brought Christ into the picture.

In an effort to define this unfathomable concept, Philip Yancey says that grace means there is nothing we can ever do to make God love us more. Grace means there is nothing we can ever do to make God love us less.[4] Only Christianity dares to extend this gift from a God who is holy to a people who are completely, utterly, repeatedly unworthy. God gives us this gift through Christ alone.

But you must come empty-handed. Hebrews 6 says we must grab onto the gift with *both hands*. Let go of the sin. If it is pornography, tell a friend who can help you let go. If it is a girl, let go, my friend. Let go today. If God has her in store for your future, he will bring her back. Let go of the memories. Let go of everything you grasp onto. Let go of the shame.

Grab onto the grace.

At the 2000 Christian Bookseller's Convention, the senior pastor of the Moody Memorial Church in Chicago, Erwin Lutzer, told a story that gave me courage to embrace that grace.

"**Grace** means there is *nothing* we can **ever do** to make God **love us more.** Grace means there is *nothing* we can ever do to make God **love us less.**"

PHILIP YANCEY
What's So Amazing About Grace

While in Washington, D. C., he'd befriended a secret service agent who'd offered him a unique tour of the White House, which would include access to the Oval Office. Of course, Lutzer accepted.

The next day the secret service agent took him to the gates of the White House. There the security guard looked Lutzer up and down with scrutiny; he began to step in front of him. As he did, the secret service agent stepped between them and said, **"He's with me."**

Through the gates they went, Lutzer with a little extra bounce in his step.

They came to the doors of the great White House. Men in black stood vigilantly guarding the access. They cautiously scrutinized Lutzer. "He's with me," said the security guard.

They walked through the finely decorated halls toward the Oval Office. As they arrived at the door to the highly secured office, they were again greeted with a stern security officer.

"He's with me," stated the secret service friend once more.

And with a smile, Erwin Lutzer was welcomed into the office of the President of the United States.

Overwhelmed with the enormity of it all, Lutzer could not help but think how much more fantastic it would be the day that he was given access to the throne of grace. He's sure that Jesus will meet him at the pearly gates where angels vigilantly guard the holy heavenlies. Though Lutzer, like all of us, may cower at the thought of making it through, when he arrives at that gate he will hear Jesus say, "He's with Me." [5]

The most deviant of murderous criminals who've come to Jesus Christ as Savior will hear the same sweet words as Billy Graham: "He's with *Me*!" How powerfully freeing that is to me, especially since I've always sort of feared that we'd be brought into heaven alphabetically and, with a name like Gresh, I'd be right behind Billy Graham!

He's with me!

That story lit a passion in me.

Does it in you?

If the enemy tries to trash you with shame, just step aside. Let the Savior of the world announce the truth as He looks at you just as you are and proudly announces,

"He's with Me!"

Sexual Integrity Challenge

Come. Come to the Savior right now. Get on your knees and picture that vilest moment from your life. Imagine Jesus coming into it and holding you, comforting you, forgiving you, and lovingly leading you away from it. Come. Get on your knees right now and grab onto grace with both hands.

If you're finding yourself thirsty with an uncertainty about all of this, maybe it's because you've never come to the Savior before. At least, not truly. There is no greater thirst quencher than Jesus Christ. When you confess your sins to Him and ask Him from this day forward to be the compass of your life, you become brand new. If you've never done that, don't waste one minute. He's waiting to embrace you.

NOTES

1. John Bradshaw, *Healing the Shame that Binds You*, (Deerfield Beach, Florida: Health Communications: 1988), 10.
2. Revelation 12:10.
3. Luke 15:11–20.
4. Philip Yancey, *What's So Amazing About Grace?* (Grand Rapids: Zondervan: 1997), 70.
5. Erwin Lutzer, "He's With Me," address to the Christian Booksellers Convention, New Orleans, 9 July 2000.

Strategy #5b:

run with the Spirit

[God's grace] teaches us to say "No" to ungodliness and wordly passions, and to live self-controlled, upright and godly lives in this present age, while we wait for the blessed hope—the glorious appearing of our great God and Savior, Jesus Christ.

TITUS 2:12–13

Strategy #5b

run with the Spirit

I glanced over my journal entries from the past few days.

4/12/2000

"Lord, teach me self-control and help me to put the values of the Cross above the value of ego."

4/13/2000

"Lord, help me to hold my tongue and to seek Your vision. Lord, help me to spend more time with You."

4/14/2000

"May the words of my mouth and the meditation of my heart be acceptable in Your sight, O Lord."

I'm not going to win a Pulitzer Prize for that writing, I thought.

But they were consistent attempts to ask God to control my day. I didn't have an entry like that for today. I'd started today with every intention of making it a great one, but I'd forgotten to ask God to control me. I scribbled today's entry.

4/15/2000

"I consider myself to have fallen tonight."

That's about all I had to say. A few hours ago I'd allowed my mind to wander. It was not a significant moment of sin, but I'd proven that I was incapable of controlling myself. No matter what tricks I tried to keep myself living right, I could not do it alone.

X-X-X-X-O-O-O-O

I spend a lot of time trying to get my act together, but inevitably I'm not that good at it. Why? It's not my job to get my act together. That's God's job. I can't come close to being able to do it. I found a story that helps me remember this.

There was a man digging ditches during a hot summer day in Texas. After he had worked for several hours, a buddy said, "Why is it we're over here breaking our backs for minimum wage, while the president of the company makes a six-figure salary for practicing his golf putting skills in an air-conditioned office?"

"I'm going to find out," the man said, throwing down his shovel. He marched toward the office building that housed the company's executive suites. In a few minutes he was standing before the company president. "Why do you make so much money for doing hardly any work, while I dig ditches and make so little?"

The company president flashed a friendly smile and said, "Come on over here, and I'll show you." He then held out his hand and said, "Hit my hand with your fist."

The worker hauled off and swung at the president's hand with all of his might. Just as his fist was about to make contact, the president moved his hand, and the ditch digger's fist slammed into the brick wall behind the president. As the ditch digger yelled in pain, the president said, "That's why I'm the president and you're a ditch digger."

The worker returned to his buddy, who asked, "What did he tell you?"

"I'll show you," the worker said as he lifted his hand in front of his face. "Hit my hand as hard as you can!"[1]

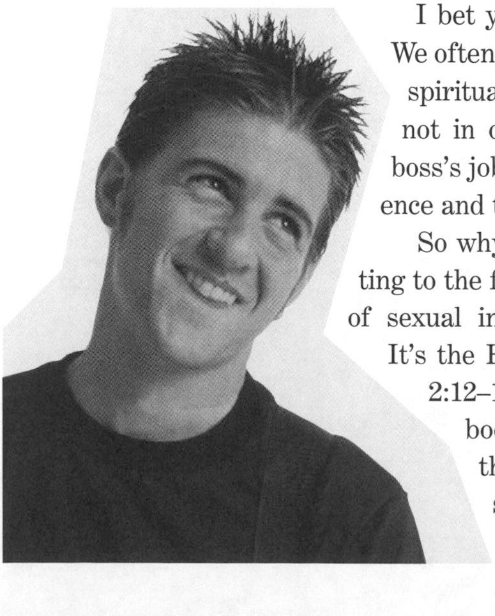

I bet you can visualize the rest of that story! We often try to do things in our spiritual lives that are just not in our job description. You can't do your boss's job. It's his job! You don't have the experience and training and wisdom.

it's his job!

So why do we have such a hard time submitting to the fact that we are incapable of living a life of sexual integrity based on our own strength? It's the Holy Spirit's job to do that in us. Titus 2:12–13 are the verses we started this whole book with. (Hey, I'm glad you've hung in there with me.) Those verses are the secret to living a life of sexual integrity. They say that "[God's grace] teaches us to say 'No' to ungodliness and worldly passions, and to live self-controlled, upright and godly lives." Only by God's power, displayed through the Holy Spirit in us, can we attain sexual integrity.

I've spent a lot of time giving you some practical ideas to help you avoid temptation. I believe these things will help you to not be that poor dude on the book cover whose face is smacked helplessly against the goalpost. I've encouraged you to:

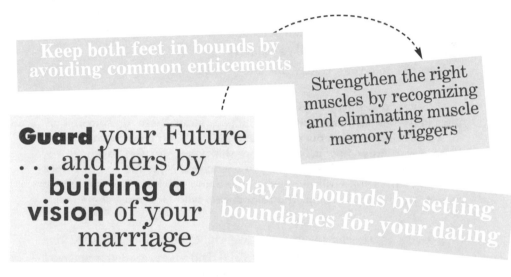

Keep both feet in bounds by avoiding common enticements

Strengthen the right muscles by recognizing and eliminating muscle memory triggers

Guard your Future . . . and hers by **building a vision** of your marriage

Stay in bounds by setting boundaries for your dating

These things are proven to be risk reducers. Sexual temptation won't show up quite as much if you build these things into your life but if it does, then what? It's the power of the Holy Spirit that will rescue you every single time.

The Holy Spirit's presence is what successfully directs you to be the guy on the cover who's sliding in for a beautiful touchdown. He's uninhibited by the crowd. He's clearing the goalpost. He's victorious.

That's what God wants for you in your sexual life. He wants you to slide past all the sick substitutes for sex that this world offers. He wants you to score in His time and in His way so that the victory is fabulous and fulfilling. Of all the training and practice you do, this is the most important. It's time to get close to the Coach. Only when you do this will you be ready to play to win in the game of sexual integrity. I have three practical ideas to help you do that.

Every morning ask the Holy Spirit to help you live right.

As you see above, my journal entries are rarely eloquent. Most often, they are pleas for God to just guide me and help me. I've learned that if I don't just stop and stand before God, my days quickly become out of control . . . and so do I. I'm not really talking about devotions or studying the Bible. Those things are a part of it—a huge part of it—but too many times we even let that be a part of what we "do" to live right. Lots of things we do can help, but not apart from just being filled with the Holy Spirit, and that takes stillness.

In *Experiencing God*, Henry Blackaby wrote:

> **We are a doing people.** We always want to be doing something. Once in a while someone will say, "Don't just stand there, do something."
>
> I think God is crying out and shouting to us, "Don't just do something. Stand there. Enter into a love relationship with Me. Get to know Me. Adjust your life to Me. Let Me love you and reveal Myself to you as I work through you." A time will come when the doing will be called for, but we cannot skip the relationship. The relationship with God must come first.[2]

Only God's Spirit can teach us to live right. Did you take time this morning to build your relationship with God? Did you stop doing and just stand there so that His Holy Spirit could fill you?

Be prepared to face temptation.

Don't expect the presence of the Holy Spirit in your life to be an automatic one-way ticket from temptation. It wasn't for Christ. In Matthew 3, we see Jesus being baptized by John and blessed by His Father. At that moment, the Holy Spirit came upon Him. It'd be a nice scene in the movies. The picture would be softly blurred, there would be violins playing, the background, and an angelic choir humming.

Then, in Matthew 4:1, we're ripped away from that safe place. It says that "Jesus was led by the Spirit into the desert to be tempted." The Holy Spirit actually led Jesus into that place of turmoil and temptation.

It's the Holy Spirit's job to make you holy. That means He has to work out every little impurity in your life. In chapter 5, we talked about the Spiral Mountain. Well, meet your Tour Guide, the Holy Spirit! He wants to see you make it to the top and become pure and holy. He knows that means you have no choice but to be led past the temptation. Frightening thought, huh? What's a guy to do? Run back into the presence of the Holy Spirit . . . and fast!

Return to Him at the moment of temptation.

Even though the Holy Spirit may allow you to face temptation, He really does want you to get *past* that temptation and not to be smacked face first into it. How? There's only one way. Return to God in prayer the moment you detect temptation. Best-selling author Bruce Wilkinson wrote candidly about a time when he had to do this. He was leaving Chicago after a week of meetings at Moody Bible Institute. He was tired and had just asked the Lord to take him home temptation-free.

"Oh Lord," I pleaded. "I have no resistance left. I'm completely worn out in Your service. I can't cope with temptation. Please keep evil from me today."

On the plane, he got stuck in a middle seat. The man on his left pulled out a pornographic magazine. So, Bruce looked the other way only to have the other guy pull out his own porno mag! Bruce wrote:

> **At that moment,** I didn't have it in me to ask them to change their reading material. I closed my eyes. "Lord," I prayed. "I can't cope with this today. Please chase evil far away!"
>
> Suddenly the man on my right swore, folded up his magazine, and put it away. I looked at him to see what had prompted his action. Nothing, as far as I

Joe White on the Power of the Holy Spirit

BOB: What kind of help does a guy need to overcome sexual temptation?

JOE: The biggest help is the power of the Holy Spirit. For a guy, the desire to have sex with a girl is stronger than anything else in the world except the power of the Holy Spirit.

BOB: Being filled with the Holy Spirit is sometimes hard for a guy to understand. Are there guidelines to accomplishing that?

JOE: What works is every morning asking the Lord to be your Lord and asking Him to be your Holy Spirit. It is a spiritual battle. I don't care what a guy does of the flesh. He can set all the goals in the world; if a guy is doing it in the flesh, he is going to fail.

could tell. Then the man on the left looked at him, swore loudly, and closed up his magazine too. Again, I could find no apparent reason for his decision.

We were over Indiana when I began laughing uncontrollably. They both asked me what was so funny.

"Gentleman," I said, "you wouldn't believe me if I told you!" [3]

Ha! What a battle. What a victory. Bruce ran right into the arms of his Savior and was rescued. Why? Because every day Bruce invites the presence of the Holy Spirit to guide him should temptation arrive. Every morning Bruce prays that God would "keep him from evil" based on 1 Chronicles 4:10. That's what we have to do every day. If we stay in the presence of the Holy Spirit, He keeps leading us back to the Cross for more power.

Do you find that hard to believe? Maybe you've been defeated so many times by lust that this just seems too simpleminded. I can identify. I've been there, but I can tell you who that lie comes from. It's from Satan who accuses you and makes you feel incapable of reaching out with both hands for the grace of God. But don't believe that liar. Reach! Reach out for the grace of God. Reach out for His power that's given us through the Holy Spirit.

Reach every day.
Reach for God's grace.
Grab it with both hands.

Are You Thirsty?

Are you ever thirsty? I mean, spiritually, thirsty? The source that we thirst for is found in a Savior who said He gives living water.[4] We come shivering in fear. We should. I do. I am afraid to drink of that refreshing water because I feel unworthy of being in His presence. But His presence is the only place where I can find what I need.

"Are you not thirsty?" said the Lion.

"I'm dying of thirst," said Jill.

"Then drink," said the Lion.

"May I . . . could I . . . —would you mind going away while I do?" said Jill.

The Lion answered this only by a look and a very low growl. And as Jill gazed at its motionless bulk, she realized that she might as well have asked the whole mountain to move aside for her convenience.

The delicious rippling noise of the stream was driving her nearly frantic.

"Will you promise not to—do anything to me, if I do come?" said Jill.

"I make no promise," said the Lion.

Jill was so thirsty now that, without noticing it, she had come a step nearer.

"Do you eat girls?" she said.

"I have swallowed up girls and boys, women and men, kings and emperors, cities and realms," said the Lion. It didn't say this as if it were boasting, nor as if it were sorry, nor as if it were angry. It just said it.

"I daren't come and drink," said Jill.

"Then you will die of thirst," said the Lion.

"Oh dear!" said Jill, coming another step nearer. "I suppose I must go and look for another stream then."

"There is no other stream," said the Lion.[5]

there is no other stream

Sexual Integrity Challenge

Stay. In the last chapter I encouraged you to come to the Savior. Now, I beg you to do the tough work of staying near to Him. That's not easy. It requires unending discipline. Will you prayerfully consider committing to praying this prayer—or one like it—every day? This prayer is written from Scripture. I believe that when we pray using Scripture it is a power-packed petition to our God.

Lord, I submit myself to You today. Please help me to resist the devil and cause him to flee from me. As I come near to You in this moment, please come near to me for this day. By Your grace teach me to say no to any temptation that he would bring my way, and help me to live a godly, self-controlled, upright life. *In the name of Jesus Christ.* **Amen**

(FROM JAMES 4:7–8; TITUS 2:12)

☐ Yes, I want to stay close to my Savior.
I commit to praying this prayer consistently!

SIGNED ______________________________ DATE ______________

NOTES

1. Bill Perkins, *When Good Men Are Tempted* (Grand Rapids: Zondervan, 1997), 100.
2. Henry Blackaby and Claude V. King , *Experiencing God Youth Edition* (Nashville: Broadman, 1994), page 16.
3. Bruce Wilkinson, *The Prayer of Jabez* (Sisters: Ore.; Multnomah, 2000), 65–66.
4. John 4:10
5. C.S. Lewis, *The Silver Chair* (New York: Macmillan, 1953), 16–17.

CHAPTER 15

Strategy #6:

choose the right Teammates

This is my life work: helping people understand and respond to this message. It came as a shear gift to me . . . God handling all of the details . . . I was the least qualified of any of the available Christians. **God saw to it that I was equipped.**

EPHESIANS 3:7–8
(*The Message*; EMPHASIS ADDED)

CHAPTER 15

Strategy #6

choose the right Team·mates

I felt like death warmed over. I'd spent the entire day in bed nursing the flu. It was a lousy way to spend a birthday. Tonight was accountability group, but there was no way . . .

The phone rang. It was Troy.

"You want me to drive?" he said.

"Hey, man," I pleaded. "I'm sick. Real sick."

"Are you dead?" asked Troy. I could tell he was enjoying this.

"I'll pick you up," he said.

Troy VanLiere, Tony Bahr, Kevin Carlisle and myself had been an accountability group for several months now. Missing was not an option.

I dragged myself to the bathroom. One look in the mirror scared me. I had a nasty shadow of a beard, dark circles under my eyes, and my hair looked like I'd stuck my finger in an electrical socket.

"Troy wants to force me to go?" I said out loud. "Let him enjoy the view!"

I pulled a sweatshirt over my T-shirt. I still had my very old, thinning pajama bottoms on. They had a nice, big hole ripped in the seat.

A few minutes later I heard Troy's horn blaring from the driveway.

"Whew! Are you really going like that?" Troy asked when I'd made it to the car.

I just frowned at him. He gave me the typical Troy grin and then drove us to Tony's house.

At accountability group everyone seemed shocked to see me looking like that. It wasn't really that they were shocked that I looked sick or that they were shocked that I came like that. There was some kind of sly, sick smile hidden behind their looks of astonishment.

After fifteen or twenty minutes of miserable, stuffy-headed prayer time, Tony tried to get us to all go to the kitchen of his huge house for a snack.

I dragged myself out of my comfy leather chair and away from the cherry paneled den. I padded through the hallway–feeling the breeze through the hole in my pajamas once again. I turned the corner to the kitchen.

"Surprise! Happy Birthday!" shouted a handful of people.

I surveyed the room. There was the bank president, my doctor, my pastor, business clients, and church friends. Just about anyone I'd definitely hope not to see me with my electric hairdo and fanny peephole was there.

I fumed for a brief moment and then started to laugh at it all.

"Well, it's a good thing my doctor's here," I joked. And the party went on, because you just don't miss accountability group. Not for anything. Not because it's your birthday. Not because you're sicker than a dog and not because you look like a bum.

XXXX-OOOO

Sorry, that's illegal!!!

On November 17, 1985, William "Refrigerator" Perry executed a decidedly illegal play on behalf of his team, the Chicago Bears. Though a 320-pound appliance on the Bear's defensive line, he was well known for the handful of times he carried the ball, knocking the other team's defenders into the next county. On one cool November day, the Refrigerator carried much more than the ball. He carried Hall of Famer Walter Payton. The ball was on the Dallas Cowboys' 2-yard line when Bears Coach Mike Ditka sent Perry in to block for Payton. Payton took a handoff, but the Cowboy's defensive line was seemingly impenetrable. So, Perry decided to carry the team . . . quite literally. He picked Payton up and toted him to the end zone. The rules didn't allow it, but the fans roared with love for the play.

A Friend When You Need Him

Sometimes, it takes a friend to get you through. I'm not talking about the kind of friend that you play football with or cut up with in class. I'm talking about the friend that knows your intimate secrets. Might very well have a Fruit of the Loom wedgie-battle trophy or two, but there has been or frequently is an intimacy in the friendship. You have some times of quiet conversation, when you talk about your dreams, your goals, and even your fears and failures. There is a love between you.

hold it! hold it right there!

Hold it! Is this getting girlie?

No, this is not girlie! David was as tough as they come. In fact, he was tough right from the start. Who else volunteered to take out the Philistine's Goliath? No one. They were too chicken. David went on to fight for King Saul, and David killed his "tens of thousands." Of course, that made the king jealous. David needed a place to hide. Saul was on a rampage. So, David pretended to be a "psycho" to get into the gates of the Philistines, his gravest enemies, where he eventually asked their king for protection from Saul.[1] Gutsy! He must have made a pretty skillful case; he got that protection. Here's a man's man.

And yet, David had deep, intimate friendships with men. I think we can take a lesson from two of his friendships.

Do you have a Jonathan?

Jonathan was probably watching his father and learning to be somewhat "kinglike" so that he could one day take the throne. During that time he probably saw David playing the harp for his half-mad father. He saw David fight Goliath. He saw his father commend David.

real men have deep friendships

Right away, the race was on for the king's affection, right? No. Instead, Jonathan expresses his love for David.

"After David had finished talking with Saul, Jonathan became one in spirit with David, and he loved him as himself" (1 Samuel 18:1).

They became one in spirit. That's how the Bible puts it. He didn't just laugh and hang with David. He was intimate with him. He loved him; Jonathan made a covenant with David because he loved him. When he did, he gave David his royal robe and tunic. At that moment, he was symbolically sacrificing his own future and saying, "It's cool. You can be the king!" A "Jonathan" kind of friend is one who willingly sacrifices to see the other person benefit. Do you have a friend like that? Are you a friend like that?

David entered into the covenant also because of love. He loved Jonathan.

There are no secrets in a friendship like this. Somehow Jonathan knew David would be king. He also knew his father would not let that happen if he could help it. Betraying his father, Jonathan warned David and saved his life.

Do you have a friend who is a Jonathan?

A "Jonathan" is a friend who
is a peer
loves you
knows your secrets
sacrifices for your benefit

After the death of Jonathan, David lamented, "I grieve for you, Jonathan my brother; you were very dear to me. Your love for me was wonderful, more wonderful than that of women."[2] More wonderful than that of women? That was an intimate, godly friendship.

These kinds of friendships are hard to find. Very hard. They require you to be intimate. They have to weather nasty times and horrid truth. I've been blessed to have a few friends whom I consider to be Jonathans. One sticks out as a guy who'd take a hit for me. His name is Troy VanLiere. You've met him in several of my personal stories. We've been in business together and had our ups and downs. But still we are friends. He knows my weaknesses and still loves me.

Do you have a Jonathan?

Do you have a Nathan?

Sometimes the friend we turn to must be older and wiser than us. David found that kind of friendship and accountability in the prophet Nathan. David ran to Nathan for advice many times. Though he was the king, he was not above seeking wise counsel.

There were no secrets here, either. At one point we find David sitting in his beautiful house when the idea came to him that his place was nicer than God's. The ark of the covenant was in a tent, and he was in this house adorned in gold. So he hatched a plan to build God's house. It would become his heart's great desire. He wasted no time in running to Nathan for advice.

Why? Because Nathan was his older, wiser accountability partner. Even David's biggest dream was not going to be kept from Nathan.

Now, Nathan wasn't perfect. He goofed when he first advised David about the temple. He told him to go ahead and build! But because he sought God's wisdom to live rightly, he was quickly corrected. Later that night, God quickened his heart, and Nathan had to return to the king, his friend, with new advice. God did not want David to have the honor of building the temple. No doubt that truth hurt. No doubt Nathan hated saying it. And David must have hated hearing it. But a "Nathan" tells it like it is.

Again, there were no secrets. David's life was vulnerable to Nathan. And when David had sex with Bathsheba, another man's wife, Nathan called him on it. There weren't any words wasted there, either. Nathan knew David had a sensitive heart. So, he told David a story. He told David about a man who had many sheep and hosted many feasts. Then Nathan mentioned another man, who had only one lovely sheep and that it was dear to him. The man with many sheep swept down into the valley, Nathan explained, and stole the lone sheep from the other man.

"What should we do?" Nathan now asks King David.

David is infuriated and immediately thinks death, punishment, protection, vengeance!

Nathan stands firm and says, "You are that man!"

David is stricken with grief and repentance.

find your
Nathan.
be a
Nathan.

Do you have a friend who is a Nathan?

A "Nathan" is a friend who

is older and wiser

loves you

is seeking God's wisdom *(though he may not be perfect)*

tells it like it is

knows your secrets

Nathans can be just as hard to find as Jonathans. I've had a few in my life, and I've found that I can't rely on just one. Maybe that's because it takes more than one to keep me straight.

George Gruendel has been one of my best Nathans. He was my Nathan in business. Graying and balding and relaxed, here was a guy who knew what intimacy is. He'd come into my business faithfully, even though he rarely got anything in return. He'd play games with my staff, which turned out to be insightful learning experiences. He'd take me to lunch and force me to look at problems I wanted to ignore. He'd invite me and my family to his rustic home in the woods to watch his bees or catch fish in his pond. He taught me serenity and to not take life too seriously. He helped me to see things I didn't want to notice.

Rick Taylor is another one of my Nathans. He vulnerably let me into his own spiritual struggles and invited me to learn from him. He was faithful about praying with me and for me and telling it like it is in the arena of sexual temptation.

Do you have a Nathan?

Are You a Jonathan . . . Are You a Nathan?

You know, someone just might need *you*. You need to be a Jonathan and a Nathan. Whether you are thirteen or thirty-three, there is someone you can mentor.

Recently Dannah and I took a leap and moved our family back to our hometown of State College, Pennsylvania. It was a bittersweet move as we said good-bye to dear friends.

The move was particularly hard on Robby, who was entering fourth grade and felt established in his "home state" of Missouri. The worst part of it all was watching him say good bye to his best friends, twins Nick and Jon Rodriguez. But God had a Nathan waiting for Robby in Pennsylvania—T. J. Struble. T. J. was probably fifteen at the time. His mom worked with Dannah's mom, and he was active in our new church's youth group. A few days after we arrived, he called and said "I'd like to take Robby fishing." The next day, amidst packing boxes and dust, T. J. and Robby headed off for Tussey Mountain. We got a new son back that evening. Robby said T. J. had talked to him about meeting new friends. That was a huge issue for our little nine-year-old. For the first time since we'd moved, he was excited and talkative.

T. J. stills singles Robby out at church, comes over some nights to watch movies with Robby or to play Nintendo when Dannah and I are going out. He might not even know it, but he is a Nathan to Robby. I am grateful.

You are someone's Nathan. And you are someone's Jonathan. Put your excuses, sins, imperfections, and insecurities aside. God can use you in spite of all of that.

That's a little hard for me to swallow sometimes. Me? I am not worthy of writing this book. And yet, we see Paul expressing this same feeling in Ephesians. "This is my life work: helping people understand and respond to this message. It came as a sheer gift to me . . . God handling all of the details. . . . I was the least qualified of any of the available Christians. God saw to it that I was equipped." He felt like the least qualified. Join the club.

Sexual Integrity Challenge

Who is your Jonathan? (If you don't have a Jonathan, who can you ask today?)

Who is your Nathan? (If you don't have a Nathan, who could you ask to be one?)

NOTES:
1. 1 Samuel 18:6–11, 28–29; 21:10–13
2. 2 Samuel 1:26

CHAPTER 16

Strategy #7:

develop your Dad

Strategy #7

develop your Dad

A family heritage is powerful. Whether you live in the lap of luxury or in the ghetto, you are guaranteed to inherit some things from your family. Some of them will be great blessings. (I got my dad's thick hair and my mom's sense of humor.)

Some of the things you inherit will not be as welcomed. Exodus 20:5 says that the sins of our fathers are passed on to the children "to the third and fourth generation." Psychologists from all walks of faith agree that we humans tend to inherit the sins of our fathers (and mothers). From the homes of hot tempers come more hot tempers. From the homes of selfish people come more selfish little people. From the homes of alcoholics come alcoholics. The prognosis is frightening for some of us.

I'd known from such an early age that lust was a powerful force in my life. I didn't know why. I thought something was wrong with me. By God's grace I had come to a knowledge of Jesus as my Lord and Savior when I was five. So, when I began to be tempted sexually, I spent every day fighting against those desires because I knew acting out on them was wrong according to God's Word. It wasn't until I was an adult that I understood why the fight for me was so strong.

During my twenties I began to understand my family heritage. Over the past eight years I've been able to put the story together. I come from a legacy of sexual recklessness. I don't know exactly how far back it goes, but I suspect further than I know. I also know that staying on the path the men ahead of me walked will take me in the opposite direction of God's intended plan for my life.

The struggle for lust is one that every single man will face. You are not immune to it, but it can become extremely difficult to win the battle if you aren't helped by your family. By God's grace, I am building a new legacy for my son to inherit. Why? Because the family heritage is one of the greatest indicators of sexual sickness or sexual integrity. Ted Roberts, a pastor from Oregon who has developed strategies to fight sexual addictions, concludes that sexual addiction is, in fact, a family system or a way of dealing with life.[1] That certainly seems to be the case in my family. If you look closely, you'll probably find the same thing in your family . . . for good or for bad.

build a new legacy

There is exciting news in all this sad stuff. The chances are pretty good that with a little work you have a father who will help you live a life of sexual integrity. I like to call this "double covering" the opponent. The opponent—Lust—is a Goliath. If he were a literal body on a football field, the coach would not hesitate to call for double cover—you know, two guys teaming against a tough opponent. I want to encourage you to invite your dad to "line up" beside for a victory that you'll celebrate for all of your life. (Just wait till you get married to start the celebration, OK?)

God can break the bondage of generational sin

What's the Big Deal About My Dad?

The most powerful description of God in the Scriptures is "Father." Many of us view God as an angry father who will do good for us only if we beg, and maybe He won't even respond then. We consider prayer to be this begging and pleading with God to give us the littlest scraps of happiness. This makes prayer exhausting. Imagine a relationship such as a cranky boss or angry coach who never gives anything without being begged and praised.

This is not how God is. He blesses us with all kinds of things. He's not keeping count of our devotions any more than a loving father judges his son on how many goals he scores. My love for my son Robby is unconditional, and although I take him through exercises that are necessary for him to progress and learn, I bless him as much as I can at all times, and I love him unconditionally. At his worst, I would love him no less. I accept him for who he is, not for what he can do for me. God does the same thing. Prayer is conversing with Him. He never forsakes me, but holds me and cherishes me like a father loves his son.

All of us need the blessing of a father's love. Dannah's dad, Dan Barker, is a father who has exemplified the father blessing in an extraordinary manner. Through the years, I know he has blessed Dannah and his son, Darin. Since the family has grown, he's included me, his soon-to-be daughter-in-law Cheryl and, of course, his grandchildren in the blessing. This past New Year's Eve we were all invited to a mysterious dinner. No one was told why, but only immediate family members were allowed to attend. That's unusual in a home where "everyone" is always invited. We all came with overwhelming curiosity.

After dinner, Dan ceremoniously presented "The Barker Family Proclamation" to us. Clearing his throat he began to read. We listened with intensity. The document

A Kick In The Seat of the Pants!

Some of you have dads in your homes who are godly men who try desperately to bless you. But you cut *yourself* off from the blessing. Dads are not perfect. Many of us struggle to be intimate. I do. It is hard for me. I never saw it modeled. But I love my kids and I pray every day that I can be the kind of father that blesses them. Maybe you need to reexamine the gift you have been given in your dad.

Thank God for my dad? Yeah, right!

Have you been hurt by your dad? It can be hard to have gratitude when you can hardly even forgive your dad. It's easy to have unforgiveness in your heart if you've missed the father blessing. But if you want to move on, you need God's power. To get God's power, you have to forgive. The Bible tells us that God can't even hear our prayers if we have unforgiveness in our hearts. Forgiving your dad is a big part of healing and crucial to your ability to begin a new heritage. Forgive your father for never protecting you. Forgive him for embarrassing you. Forgive him for not spending time with you. Forgive him for missing your games. Forgive him for loving his work so much. Forgive him for not making you feel loved. You even need to forgive him if he's abused you. Don't expect forgiveness to change him. Forgiveness is about what God does in and through you. Remind yourself that "Though my father and mother forsake me, the Lord will receive me."[2]

recounted the growth of the family through the years, the wonderful accomplishments of the year 2000, and the hopes of the future. The Proclamation ended with, "Now therefore, Walter Daniel and Kay Francis Barker, parents of the Barker family, do hereby confirm the blessings of our generation on each and every member of the Barker family now and in the future to include those members of the Barker family yet to be conceived but known only to God and do declare that the year 2000 was an exceptional blessing for the Barker family and should be commemorated in this proclamation and noted forever." He ended by saying, "These truly are the good ol' days!"

Wow! I felt so amazed. I was a part of this. I had someone watching me and believing in me. There were expectations for my future and someone to cheer me on to meet those expectations. I felt blessed. That's the father blessing.

The father blessing is not usually quite so formal. Usually you see the father blessing when a dad watches a son play ball with a look on his face that says, "That's my son!" You'll see it when a father talks to his young son about "what you want to be when you grow up" or later on helps him plan for college. It's even being offered when a father is teaching his son to use all the tools in the toolbox and says, "Good job."

Ultimately, the father blessing says two things. In Matthew 3 we see God the Father modeling the father blessing for us. Jesus is baptized and God the Father comes down and says, "This is my Son, whom I love; with him I am well pleased." That's what we all need from a dad. We need to hear him say, 'He is *mine!*" and "I am *proud!*" Each of us deeply desires to know that blessing.

Missing the Blessing

You might be saying, "How do I know if I've missed the father blessing?" Let me give you three common ways guys are missing the blessing today.

A big reason a lot of guys miss the blessing of a father is because they don't live with their dads. Divorce and out-of-wedlock pregnancies separate many of you from your dads. In *Fatherless America*, David Blankenhorn states that about 40 percent of kids do not even live with their dads. Some dads do the best they can in those circumstances, but Blankenhorn would strongly argue that even in the best cases, divorce leaves a deep longing that I would say can be equated with a missed father blessing. It is hard to know a man we don't live with.[3] (How can we know their blessings if we don't even know *them?*)

A second reason a lot of guys miss the blessing of a father is because he is totally non-intimate. I believe this is a form of neglect. Maybe their dads are alcoholics, sex addicts, or workaholics. If you live with a dad who is non-present (there physically, but not mentally) or one who is just rarely home, you might be experiencing this kind of a missed blessing. I knew my dad was nuts about me, but I did not know his blessing. He was there physically, but he was very rarely there mentally and emotionally. I believe he did the best he knew.

A final reason might be outright abuse. They may verbally abuse them. That was John's experience, reports Ted Roberts.

> **John's face lit up a little,** because he had been a superb athlete. He told me of the joy of winning a state championship. He earned a full scholarship to college because of his skills. After the championship game was over, he was voted the Most Valuable Player. He went forward and received the MVP trophy, with his father standing beside him. It should have been a red-letter day. I asked John what his father said to him afterward. The joy dropped off his face and tears streamed down his cheeks. He could barely say the words: "He told me someone else should have received it. I wasn't that good."[4]

John was familiar with outright verbal abuse.

I know a guy who has been deeply affected by just *witnessing* abuse. He and his brothers and sisters would often sneak out of the house at night when their dad started beating their mom. They themselves were not physically abused, but the damage was just as bad. Imagine sneaking out of the house in your pj's as a young child and wondering if your mom would be alive when you returned the next day? Imagine wondering where you would go at three in the morning to sleep and feel safe? Perhaps you don't have to imagine. Perhaps you know that fear.

Abuse can also be direct physical or sexual abuse. I wish it were less common than it is. Oh, I hope you have not known that pain. If you have, let me say this "It was not your fault."

(Be sure to see the letter in the appendix from a survivor of child abuse.) I wrestle with whether the worst part of it is the actual abuse or the deep, painful scar your dad left in you when he failed to affirm you.

If you recognize yourself in any of these missed blessings, stick close. There is hope for you!

Restoring the Blessing

It is vital that we each know that blessing. It will affect all of your life, but particularly your ability to be intimate and to have a healthy sexual relationship with your wife one day. The National Center for Fathering reported that in 1997–98 the men who had purchased pornographic materials in the past year had significant father issues compared to those who had not purchased pornography in the same year. [5]

Here are two practical things I can suggest no matter what kind of dad you have.

Bless your father.

God tells us to give thanks for everything. *Everything!* Even our dads. I believe this is because when we have the clean heart that comes with being thankful, we cannot become controlled by a stronghold of bitterness and anger. We open the door for God to go to work.

When was the last time you thanked God for your dad? Have you ever done that?

Earlier I mentioned Ted Roberts. He never met his dad and was abused by his stepfather. He was desperately missing the father blessing. He came to a powerful turning point.

One day in his office he felt the Holy Spirit gently nudge him to "Give God praise for your father." He was reluctant at first, as you might be if you had been left by your father and beaten by his replacement. But he sensed God was helping him to heal the father wound in his heart. So he stood and spoke words he never thought he would. He said, "Dad, I never got to meet you. I never knew who you were, but thanks for giving me life. Hopefully, I'll get to meet you at the other end." He says it was like a dam broke as his emotions were released and he wept convulsively for the next half hour.[6]

Take a moment to thank God for your father.

Ask your spiritual father to be involved in your quest for sexual integrity.

Each of us needs a spiritual father—a guy who can lead us to a deeper relationship with God. If you have a decent dad, it's time to step up to the plate. He's probably as clumsy as I am and doesn't know when or how to bring things up like sexual temptation. He might not even know exactly how to guide you through your spiritual journey. Since our sexual integrity . . . or lack of it . . . so directly affects our spiritual journey, it is important that the subject of sexuality be a big part of your dialogue with your dad.

If you have no relationship with your father or a very poor one, let me suggest that you find either a grandfather, pastor, or older, wiser man in your church and adopt him as a spiritual dad. Let him read this chapter and tell him you need a father figure. That's a

huge step of intimacy. It takes guts. But it is necessary for you if you struggle with your relationship with your dad. There can be no excuses here!

A little request from you could be just what he needs to get things going in a good direction with your spiritual dad. (As dads, we sometimes aren't the greatest at bringing things up ourselves.) Make a formal effort to start this kind of relationship with your dad. I want to ask you to write a letter to your dad. Writing will let you readjust your attitude (and his if he needs it). You can edit and rewrite things as you go. This can be powerful. Ron Hutchcraft, the host of a great youth-oriented Christian radio show, says that a letter is "usually better said, better heard and better remembered."[7] He has seen simple letters transform families.

letters transform families

Knowing and Accepting Dad

Maybe as a little kid or young teen you watched the 1993 Disney movie *Homeward Bound: The Incredible Journey.* The movie begins with a wedding scene. Laura is getting married and her three kids are getting a new "dad." The oldest boy, Peter, is suspicious and obviously angry. Immediately following the wedding, the family leaves their home to go to San Francisco, where the new dad has a temporary job. The family's three beloved pets, one for each kid, are left with a friend who lives on a ranch. The children are disappointed, and Peter strongly resents his stepfather's action.

You know the kid-pleasing story line: The pets miss their "children" and begin the long journey to return home to them.

Most remember the movie for its talking animals and beautiful vistas as the two dogs and a cat make the "incredible journey" home, but the story's deeper than that. When the family found out about the loss and began a grueling search for them, the stepfather leads the way. Over the next few weeks, the pets show the courage and faith to find their way home. At the same time, the kids begin to embrace their new father as they see him trying to rescue their pets. Moments before the pets appear, suspicious Peter calls his new stepfather "Dad." The pets run over the hill and everyone is happy.

David Blankenhorn, founder of the Institute of American Values, sees two complementary morals in the story. Pets, when they miss those they love, can find their way back home. Children, when they are separated from a father's love, can find a new father's love. "To find their home, pets go back. To find their father, children go forward!" Blankenhorn writes.[8]

Hey, I'm as childlike as they come when you're talking about the blessing of a father. We never outgrow that.

It's time to step forward.

It's time to move aggressively toward that father blessing.

Sexual Integrity Challenge

It's time do those two things I suggested. First, take a few minutes to praise God for your dad . . . especially if you don't feel like it! Then, take just ten minutes to write that letter I suggested. You'll be glad you did.

NOTES

1. Ted Roberts, *Pure Desire* (Ventura, Calif.: Regal, 1999), 24.
2. Psalm 27:10.
3. David Blankenhorn, *Fatherless America* (New York, Basic Books, 1995), 19.
4. Roberts, *Pure Desire,* 24.
5. Promise Keepers Newsletter, Vol. I, Number 4, July-August 1998, Ken VanHyning, Obsessed and Consumed.
6. Roberts, *Pure Desire,* 24.
7. Ronald Hutchcraft, *How to Get Your Teenager to Talk to You* (Wheaton, Ill.: Victor, 1984), 50.
8. David Blankenhorn, *Fatherless America* (New York, Basic, 1995), 188

finishing Strong

> **Watch out for the Esau Syndrome,** trading away God's lifelong gift in order to satisfy a short-term appetite.
>
> HEBREWS 12:16 (*The Message*)

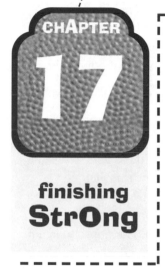

finishing StrOng

There's a story about a guy who bought a chain saw that disappointed him. He angrily took it back to the store where he'd bought it.

"They told me I could cut fifty trees a day with this thing. I worked all day long and only got five trees down," he told the salesperson.

The salesperson kindly began to look the chain saw over for problems. Then he pulled the rip cord.

"Rrrrrreer . . . rrrrrrrreer" roared the chainsaw.

"What's *that* noise?" asked the customer in wonderment!

Life's like that a lot of times. We have everything we need in our hands but we just don't use it. We make things hard because we don't apply the power of our tools.

I'd like to think that this book has offered you some useable tools. But they won't help you unless you use them and use them right. If you just read through this, you won't find the victory you're looking for. If you took time to do the integrity challenges and pray, congratulations. You've just begun to live a life of sexual integrity.

And I do mean, you've just begun!

Living this kind of life is kind of like running a marathon. Do you know how we got the word "marathon?" It all started in 490 B.C. during a great battle that took place on the plain of Marathon in Greece. A soldier named Pheidippcides was ordered to run to Athens with the news that Greece had just won the battle with Persia. Athens was twenty-five miles away! The poor guy staggered into Athens many hours later and yelled, "Rejoice! We conquer!" Then, he dropped dead.

Well, there's nothing really romantic about this, but that's how I want to end the sexual integrity story of my life. I want to run hard, just like a marathon runner. I want to run right up to the finish. And right before I plop over dead, I want to look at my wife and say, "Rejoice! We conquered!" OK, I won't say it like that. I'll probably say, "I did it. We did it. I made love to only you. Yes!" That is the greatest goal of my life.

the greatest goal of my life

We've compared the struggle to defeat sexual temptation to a football game plan, complete with strategies. But a football game only lasts four quarters, each fifteen minutes. That suggests a quick contest—more like a sprint. But in this game, no sprinting's allowed.

You're in a marathon!

Are you ready to run that hard and that long? As hard as you need to run now to avoid temptation, that's how hard you'll still need to run when you are in your thirties. And, I'm not there yet, but guys in their fifties and sixties tell me they're still running. You'll run hard all of your life for this victory.

Esau could've used some advice like that. He didn't look at life as a marathon. He looked at it as a bunch of little sprints.

In Genesis 25 we find him in an interesting position. His appetite is out of control. He's hungry. In fact, he says he might die if he doesn't get some

of his brother, Jacob's, stew. Jacob is willing to bargain with him. He'll trade Esau's birthright for a bit of stew.

Now, that doesn't mean much to you and me, but a birthright was a big deal back then. First, it meant that Esau would get *double* what Jacob got when their dad passed on his possessions.[1] More importantly, it meant that Esau would be the spiritual leader of the family.[2] Jacob had spent much time in the tents gathering knowledge about God, and he had become passionate about leading the family to Him. Esau had only a passion for the fields. Because he spent little time learning about God, he had little interest in the family faith.

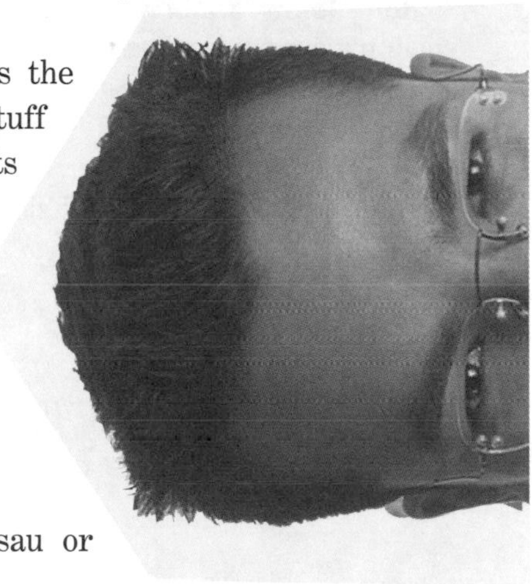

Esau makes the trade. Jacob gets the birthright to a double portion of dad's stuff and to lead the family in faith. Esau gets a full belly.

Hebrews 12:16–17 tells us to watch out for the Esau Syndrome. It warns us not to trade God's lifelong gift in order to satisfy a short-term appetite.

Could we learn a lesson from Esau or what? God wants us to know the lifelong gift of a great sexual relationship with *one* woman. But we have to wait for His timing to receive that gift. Many times along the way, your appetite will be strong. You'll be tempted to trade in the gift for a quick fix. If you spend too much time "in the fields" and not enough time with God, you'll lose your passion to go the distance.

Are you a marathon runner or a sprinter? Are you willing to go the distance to know God's lifelong gift?

I wish this were the end of my story. I wish I could say, "Hey, I made it and you can too." I can't say that because I'm still in the race. I'll be in this race until the day I die. But I intend to finish it! I want my story to end in victory kind of like the apostle Paul. I'll let him speak for both of us:

> **You've all been to the stadium and seen the athletes race.** **Everyone runs; one wins. Run to win. All good athletes train hard. They do it for a gold medal that tarnishes and fades. You're after one that's gold eternally.**
>
> **I don't know about you, but I'm running hard for the finish line. I'm giving it everything I've got. No sloppy living for me! I'm staying alert and in top condition. I'm not going to get caught napping, telling everyone else all about it and then missing out myself.**[3]

That about says it for me. Enough of this strategizing. I'm reaching out for the prize. Do you want it too?

Ready, set . . . run!

And hey, watch out for that goalpost!

NOTES
1. Deuteronomy 21:17.
2. Exodus 4:22.
3. 1 Corinthians 9:24–25, *The Message.*

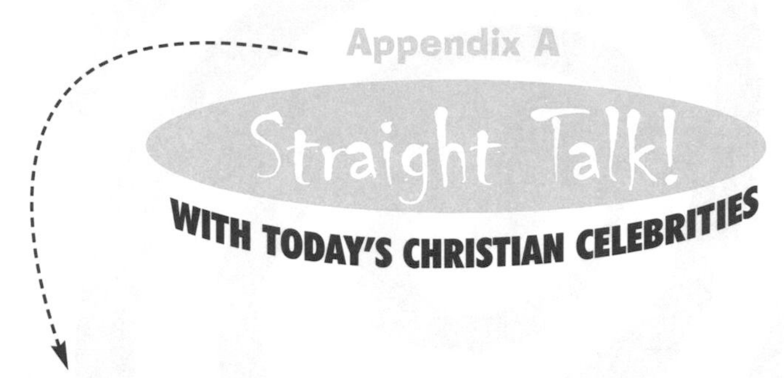

Appendix A
Straight Talk!
WITH TODAY'S CHRISTIAN CELEBRITIES

Straight Talk About Defeating Lust with **Clay Crosse**

Contemporary Christian Music Recording Artist

Clay Crosse burst onto the Christian music scene several years ago and received a Dove Award for "Best New Artist of the Year." Songs like "I Surrender All" and "He Walked A Mile" became number one singles. He was living the successful Christian life in the spotlight. When his A Different Man CD was released, I knew I had to talk with him. Along with the project, which he says is his testimony, came his public confessions about his struggle with lust. Here was a Christian man in the eye of the Christian world who was willing to be vulnerable about his struggle. I have an awesome respect for the character and tremendous obedience to God that it takes to be so transparent. I got to take an afternoon phone call from Clay during which I asked him to share candidly with me—and you—about his struggle with lust. And he did!

BOB: What brought you to a point of dealing with this?

CLAY: Well, ya know, you can deny things. For years, I didn't realize the struggle or I didn't want to think about it but *finally* a couple of years ago I took a real hard look in the mirror . . . at my life, what it was shaping up to be and where it was headed. I didn't like it. I was scared. I was scared that my marriage was going to be destroyed . . . or my ministry that God's blessed me with, the platform that I have. That's what resulted in my recommitment to Christ two years ago.

I basically cleaned up my life—the things I would watch and look at, like occasional pornography. It wasn't an addiction. It wasn't like it was something I looked at all the time. Even months or years would go by between the times I would look at it, but I would still fall for it now and then. Pretty much on a regular basis, the movies I watched, the TV shows I watched, the things I would allow into my life—I was pretty loose about it. I thought I could handle things. I mean, I am not even talking about pornography. The normal TV shows, the normal magazine articles that just push what we believe. They just became an important part of my life. I had to have a filtering system.

BOB: Can you tell us about that filtering system?

CLAY: A few years ago I would see any of the movies that came out, especially the comedies and stuff. The more they pushed it, the funnier I thought it was. I'll just use a movie for an example—a popular movie—*American Pie.* Rene and I just decided we were not going to see that. People told us, "Man, it's hilarious. You gotta go see that." Up to that point, we'd pretty much go see all the funny movies. I pushed it. That was the first time in our marriage that we really took a stand. That movie was the beginning. There have been other movies since then that we won't go see. With the Internet reviews, you can pretty much tell what you are walking into.

BOB: Dannah and I went through that with R-rated movies and stuff. I mean, it *is* funny.

CLAY: Oh yeah!

BOB: What surprises us sometimes is that people will encourage us to go see a movie like *There's Something About Mary*. Then you see it and you think "This *is* funny. I mean, there are funny scenes in there, but I shouldn't be laughing at this and I shouldn't be here."

CLAY: That's the thing. That's the hook. Even 95 percent of that movie is OK and a lot of it is funny. I did see that and it was funny. But I'm with you. I shouldn't have seen it. That's just an example of how we can be lured in.

BOB: Do you have friends who call you legalistic? How do you balance that?

CLAY: Well, we just have to have standards in our life. I think about the term

"peer pressure." It is not just for teenagers. It is for adults as well. Some people may look at my stand and say, "Come on, Clay! You've given up pornography in your life and made a rededication to Christ. These normal movies are not *that* big a deal." True, they are not to the extent of porn but they are not what we stand for. I mean, Rene and I are movie buffs. We still go to movies, but we are a lot more careful about what we see.

You know, Christians are great about saying, "It could be a lot worse." I hear parents talk about how kids listen to N'Sync and Britney Spears and they are worried about that and I almost want to tell them there are a lot worse acts out there than those, but we can only keep saying that so long. There are always worse movies, but the more you say that the more you let more stuff into your life. You just slowly lower your standards.

BOB: Even if you don't go to movies or mess around with pornography, most of us have to have a system as guys because you cannot just ignore this stuff. It's all over the billboards and TV. It *is* our culture. What keeps you on track?

CLAY: Accountability. That's huge. I do meet with an accountability partner. I know everything about him. He knows everything about me. We ask each other questions and pray for each other. Man, I highly recommend that for everybody.

BOB: A lot of guys are afraid of that because they think they are alone in this, that they are the only one struggling.

CLAY: No! The person would be alone who is not in this! The guy who says I am not tempted by, say Victoria's Secret commercials or just everything in our society, that guy—he's the one that's alone.

BOB: Are there any songs on this new project, *A Different Man*, that reflect your journey through this?

CLAY: It's pretty much a testimony album. Songs like "98." It talks about my year in 1998, which included my rededication to Christ. It says, "When I turned my back on You, You stood right there and You never left me." That's God's forgiveness right there. Even during my wandering around and straying and exploring things in my life that I shouldn't have, He was right there. He was just waiting and saying "When are you gonna come back to Me?" In 1998, He showed me that I needed to and I am so thankful to Him.

BOB: One of the lies that Satan feeds us guys says that if you struggle with this before marriage, it'll go away when you get married.

CLAY: I thought that too. I really did. For a few years it was different. I didn't want pornography in my life. Eventually it crept back in. It was probably six years into our marriage. For some guys, I am sure it's a lot sooner than that. You can't look at marriage as being your savior. Christ is our Savior. The rest is our walk and our life. It's not easy. Anybody who's married will agree to that. It's hard work. The work is worth it in the end. That's the way I look at it. It's a blessing.

Bob's Pick of Clay Crosse's CDs

A Different Man

This project is the testimony of Clay Crosse. Get it, sit down with it, and read the words as you listen to it the first time. It'll challenge you.

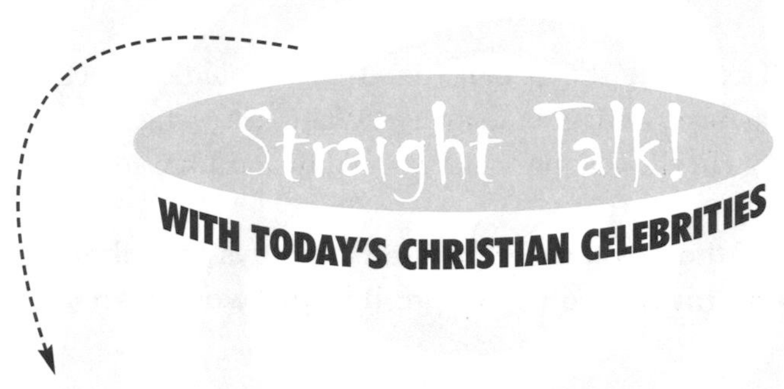

Straight Talk About What a Girl Wants

with V*Enna, the duo of Lucy Britten and Sharnessa Shelton

Christian Music Recording Artists

*I asked Dannah to find some very cool girls to talk to us about their opinions of guys and dating. She got on the "telly" to England and had a chat with the very beautiful and talented girls of the V*Enna duo, Lucy Britten and Sharnessa Shelton. Take a peek into the hearts of girls as we listen in! Hey, Sharnessa is a U. S. girl, but when you read Lucy's comments be sure to add a British accent . . . it's much cooler that way!*

DANNAH: Hey, how did you come up with the name V*Enna? Does that mean anything?

SHARNESSA: Initially, we just thought it was cute and girly, but more recently we discovered that it means "white field," which when fields turn white it means they're ready to be harvested! So we were quite excited about that as it's a huge part of what we want to see happen—a massive harvest for God!

DANNAH: Let's start with a fun question. You have met some neat guys in the music industry, I bet. Are there any guys who you've met who really stood out to you as far as being totally awesome in the way they treat girls?

SHARNESSA: I have to say that I have been so impressed with the guys we've met. All of them! The Third Day guys are so sweet! And there's a new band called Jake who are three brothers, Marty, Toby, and Josh, and their friend, Johnny. We've gotten to know them pretty well and I've been so impressed with them! There's such a purity and innocence about them—you know there's no ulterior motives. You can just be yourself and not worry about trying to impress and put your best foot forward. It's just friends hanging out together!

DANNAH: Is that something you think girls today would like? The quality of purity?

SHARNESSA: Yeah, I do. I mean purity is something God calls us all to strive for. Like in 2 Timothy 2:22, Paul tells Timothy to "run from anything that stimulates youthful lust. Follow anything that makes you want to do right. Pursue faith and love and peace, and enjoy the companionship of those who call on the Lord with pure hearts." So, basically, it just boils down to trying to be like Jesus in every area of our lives!

DANNAH: What about dating?

SHARNESSA: When I was fourteen, I read an article in Joshua Harris's magazine *New Attitude* about waiting instead of dating, and it totally struck a chord with me! I read it and was, like, "Oh my gosh! This totally makes sense!" And it's not that it's been easy, not at all! But I just knew that I wanted to wait for the one that God had for me, and give him my whole heart instead of what was left after many relationships. (Not that He can't redeem things, 'cause I TOTALLY believe He can. I've seen it happen and it's awesome!) I just really wanted to use my singleness for Him, use it as a time of growth and preparation for the future without unnecessary distractions, and just trusted that in His perfect timing He'd bring "the one" along! But I have to say that I've loved having guys as friends, it really is so cool.

I think if people thought more along the lines of treating each other for what we are—brothers and sisters in Him—there would be a lot less heartbreak. How awesome would that be if more guys and girls were looking out for each other and seeing how they could honor and protect each other, with the thought in mind that God already has someone out there for most of us!

DANNAH: Lucy? Did you date?

LUCY: I did date.

DANNAH: Can you remember some dates that were good, healthy. I mean, can dating be good?

LUCY: Yes, I believe dating can be good! As with a lot of things in life it depends how you go into it. Dating, if gone into with the right attitude, can be a time to learn how to treat a person and find out about yourself before you find your soul mate. Dating becomes unhealthy when one or both of the couple compromise their morals and give too much of themselves to that person, e.g., sleeping with them.

DANNAH: How should guys treat girls on dates?

LUCY: Girls like to be treated like they're the most beautiful girl in the world!

DANNAH: What does a girl look for when she is hoping to find the right guy?

SHARNESSA: Years ago I made a list of what I wanted in my "man" and it had like 52 items on it! Oy vey! But the top thing was that I wanted him to be totally in love with Jesus, first and foremost. Because, until you're satisfied and fulfilled in your relationship with Him, you won't be in your relationships with people—your mate in particular. And then, of course, I wanted him to be head-over-heels in love with me! To be quick, some other things were communication, integrity, honesty, masculine yet tender, romantic, respectful of his and my parents, makes me laugh, and of course, gorgeous (at least to me!)

LUCY: I believe communication is very important in a relationship. It keeps it healthy and shows respect for the other partner. I also believe selflessness is very important. The more you love someone, the more you want to give to that person, that in turn makes them feel like the most important person in the world!

DANNAH: In girls you meet, do you see a lot of hurt inflicted by guys because of selfish sex?

LUCY: I live in a rough council estate as part of a project called Eden Wythenshawe. A few Christians have moved into the area to hang out with the young people, start youth clubs and give them a chance to get off the streets. I do see a lot of pain clouded by peer pressure. It's seen as cool to do all you can with the opposite sex, but this leads to youth finding their security in guys or girls, which can be very destructive. We're trying to make these young people aware of the life they can have if they put their security in God.

Bob's Pick of V*Enna's CDs

Where I Wanna Be

*If you like the sound of Britney Spears, but don't like the message, give V*Enna a listen. Their hit single "Where I Wanna Be" is great and is followed up with more good stuff.*

Straight Talk About The Power to Overcome Sexual Temptation with Joe White

Co-host of Life on the Edge LIVE!

I've never met Joe White, but I'd sure like to. The minute I heard his slow, Texas accent, I felt relaxed. But I'm betting he knows how to have fun, too, since he's the founder of Kanakuk-Kanakomo Kamps! They're the nation's largest network of Christian camps with a reputation second to none for fun and deeply challenging spiritual experiences, including mentoring visits by some of today's top Christian athletes and celebrities. Each summer about 21,000 campers and counselors come into a deeper relationship with Christ because of this guy. You may have heard him on Focus on the Family's nationwide Life on the Edge LIVE call-in radio show for teens. (If you haven't, check it out this Saturday at http://www.family.org/lote/lotelive/.)

BOB: You wear a lot of different hats, but they are all related to youth. What is the best part of working with youth?

JOE: You know what, I had the privilege just about twenty minutes ago to lead a young man to the Lord. I like to say that America's youth are our greatest natural resource. There is nothing more exciting than being able to develop that natural resource. I have a lot of friends who are in the oil business and when they strike a gusher, they think that's the greatest thing in the world. But for me, to see the Lord be able to drill into a guy's heart and to know that'll produce a young man who's gonna follow Christ, and have a godly marriage and raise godly children and who will be a leader not only in a relationship with a girl but also our country . . . there's nothin' like that for me!

BOB: How often do you deal with sexual integrity issues with guys? Is that a prevalent thing in your ministry?

JOE: Half of our campers are guys. So, that's about 10,000. *Every* one of those guys would tell you that the biggest challenge in their life is to be sexually pure…with their mind and with their body.

BOB: What help are they getting?

JOE: It depends on how much help they want. The biggest help is the power of the Holy Spirit. I once told my wife that **for a guy, the desire to have sex with a girl is stronger than anything else in the world except the power of the Holy Spirit.** If a young man's heart is controlled by the Holy Spirit, as Ephesians 5:18 says, then the fruit of the spirit which is self-control will give him the ability to say no.

BOB: Being filled with the Holy Spirit is sometimes hard for a guy to understand . . . there are down times. Are there other guidelines or barricades that you suggest in his everyday living that you have seen to be successful?

JOE: What works is every morning asking the Lord to be your Lord and asking Him to fill you with the Holy Spirit [Ephesians 5:18]. It is a spiritual battle. I don't care what a guy does of the flesh. He can set all the goals in the world, if a guy is doing it in the flesh, he is going to fail.

The second thing is that a guy establishes his vision for what his marriage is going to be. If a young man can see that some day he's going to marry the greatest girl that ever lived—the most beautiful girl that ever lived—if he can see that when she walks down the aisle that he is going to give her his moral purity, and when she walks into the honeymoon bedroom and he desires to have nobody else in bed but her—[that's motivation.] When they kiss and they have sex, she will be the only one on his mind—he won't be seeing Miss October and Miss Eleventh Grade Girlfriend. That dream, I think is the second greatest motivation that a guy has to stay pure.

The third thing, and in that order, is that a guy sets firm boundaries. The first boundary is how far he's going to go with a girl before he's married. Based on his vision of his marriage, he sets a boundary for how far is too far. Then the second thing that a guys sets, is what are the boundaries for his eyes. Because "as a man sees, so he does." In Psalm 101:3 David says "I put nothing unclean before my eyes." Job says, " I make a covenant with my eyes not to look with lust upon a young woman" [Job 31:1 NLT]. I believe the second boundary he sets is the only person he wants to see unclothed or partially unclothed is his wife. And therefore, that's going to make my choices for movies and television clear. If there is a movie or television show where somebody else is partially unclothed then I'm going to have sex with her with my eyes. So, I have to set the boundaries there to not see that.

BOB: How do you think Jesus looks at these guys who are struggling with sexual temptation?

JOE: Well, He would say, "Guys that's why I gave My Holy Spirit, because I know you can't do it alone. And that's why I died on the cross, because I know that you'll be so upset with yourself that you'll get discouraged. The cross is there to forgive you and to let you know that 'there is now no condemnation for those who are in Christ Jesus' [Romans 8:1]. That'll give you the energy next time to say no and to know that you are loved. But I give you My Holy Spirit to give you the strength and courage to say no until you are married."

BOB: Teens rarely hear that the person from the pulpit struggled too. They don't hear that leaders, Christian musicians, Christian athletes, pastors, and people they look up to struggle with sexual temptation. All teens hear is "flee youthful lusts." It's overwhelming because it's only dealt with every thirty messages, so a guy wonders "Why do I struggle with it every day?"

JOE: Sex has always been a struggle for me and still is to this day. Without the Lord I would be a total failure. I am comfortable saying that without the Lord I'm sure I'd be the biggest mess that ever lived. Anything I do that is good is all by God's grace.

Pure Excitement

Wow! Now that's a candid guy whose example I'd like to follow. You can get more insight from him through his award-winning book, Pure Excitement. And by all means, check out his camps at www.kanakuk.com!

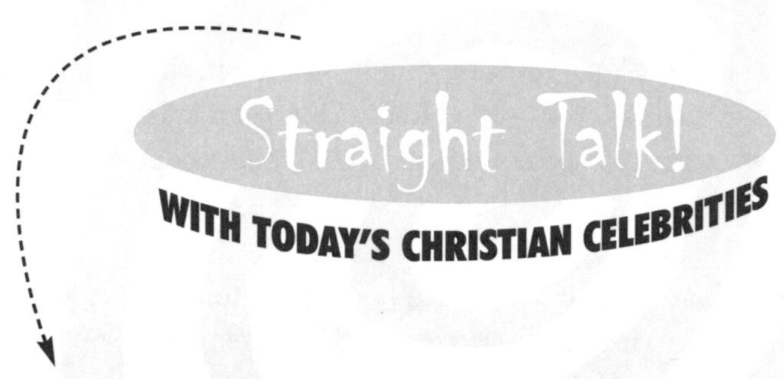

Straight Talk About Taking a Stand and Taking Care of Your Sister!

with LaRue, the brother and sister duo of Phillip and Natalie LaRue

Christian Music Recording Artists

This dynamic brother/sister singing team is passionate about the issue of purity. They've collected over 35,000 signatures to take a stand for abstinence education in public schools. And they can speak with some credibility since they're both still teenagers themselves. Join them in taking a stand by logging on to www.laruepetition.com. For now, check out the neat way Phillip helps protect his sister . . . something else he is passionate about!

BOB and DANNAH: Tell us about the LaRue Petition.

NATALIE: Well, basically it started because Philip and I wrote a song called, "Someday," which is a prayer for our future spouse. We felt compelled that we should talk about abstinence. Through doing that we really saw people's lives being touched. So we went together with a record label and management and came up with the LaRue Petition.

It's our goal to get one quarter of a million signatures on it. We are saying that we want abstinence taught in public schools as a preferred method. More than we want the government to respond we want to create public awareness.

PHILLIP: We have like 35,000 signatures.

NATALIE: We've got a long way to go. This has been really awesome for us. We're going to do it and we are going to do it until we get every last signature.

We want to inspire people. We're getting others started in their communities. No matter how hard we try, these kids know their community better than anyone else. When someone speaks out and is strong about it, it makes a difference in the community.

PHILLIP: We're actually trying to inspire people . . . to let them know they are not alone. We want to inspire them to say, "Hey, I can stand up for something I believe in." We are excited to see that happening. We also don't want to come across as "We are Christians, and so we don't have sex." We want to be sensitive to what others have experienced. What do you think, Nat?

NATALIE: We have so many friends who have made mistakes. They come to us and say, "No one ever told me that it would hurt this bad or I'd be infected for the rest of my life." We want to reach out to those people.

PHILLIP: What's really sad is that a lot of non-Christian people are saying "Hey, this makes sense." It's funny how onboard the non-Christians are with the abstinence movement. When you compare the world and church, the ratio of sexual activity is the same. It shouldn't be like that.

BOB and DANNAH: Isn't that sad?

PHILLIP: Oh, it's so sad! Something that Natalie and I try to do is to be honest and real. With God there is always a second chance. There is forgiveness. We really try, because we are teenagers, to come across as real. We don't try to say there is no temptation, because that's not the case.

Travelling and meeting all these beautiful girls is difficult for me. I don't have it all figured out but with God's grace, I can stand up. I am waiting to have sex because I think it's going to be that much more amazing with my wife. How much more incredible when she looks in my eyes and says "I've saved this for you!" I want to say that to her, too.

I've talked to other artists about this. I think the hardest thing for me is that I go through a time of condemnation when I'm walking through the mall or whatever and I see a pretty girl, I feel so weird. What you do with those thoughts, though, is what matters.

If I look up and she's gorgeous and she looks at me and I think a weird thought, I just say, "God, I turn this thought over to you." If I turn it over right away, then eventually those thoughts don't occur as much. God gives me strength. If I rely on God, that's when He really does a work in me. It really passes all understanding.

BOB and DANNAH: What's your secret to living a life of sexual integrity?

PHILLIP: Accountability is so important. I talk to my dad. I talk to other guys. These thoughts and sexual struggles happen to everybody. I really rely on my family to keep me grounded.

BOB and DANNAH: Is there anything you do to help other guys or your family live a pure lifestyle?

PHILLIP: One thing I point out is that a lot of guys don't want any man to mess with their sister but they can go out and mess with another guy's sister. If you think about it like "Hey, that's somebody else's sister or that's someone's future wife." Maybe you'll have an easier time respecting her. I'm pretty protective of Natalie. I always have been but now I'm even more. There are these guys looking up at her like she's a goddess or something.

BOB and DANNAH: Natalie, how does he protect you? How can these guys protect their sisters?

NATALIE: We try to just be more aware of when one of us is getting attention from the opposite sex. If there is flirting or something or even if there is just a bunch of guys near me, Phil doesn't desert me. He stays there and focuses the conversation. He doesn't leave me alone with guys.

BOB and DANNAH: Do you guys ever double date?

NATALIE: No, we don't. We totally should!

PHILLIP: We *totally* should! But really, we don't date a lot. We really aren't into dating just to date. I'm not going to date anyone unless I think she might be "the one." It takes some time for me to decide whether or not I will ask a girl out. We've never really been into the whole dating thing. What do ya think, Nat?

NATALIE: We don't date just to date or have a boyfriend just for the fun of it. I'm a romantic at heart. My heart gets too involved. No matter if the guy is right or not, I take the time and look for my family to agree that it is a good idea and this guy has the possibility of being in my future for life.

BOB and DANNAH: Do you see a lot of girls getting their hearts broken when they date?

NATALIE: I have seen that completely. It's not like your hormones are going on a rampage but you really desire because you care to give yourself to a guy emotionally when you date him. Sometimes a girl thinks and feels pressure to do that. Just even kissing a guy is totally giving a part of myself to him. A guy doesn't realize how much a girl is giving herself to him. It's not something to take lightly at all. You have to be careful. Care more about the girl than yourself.

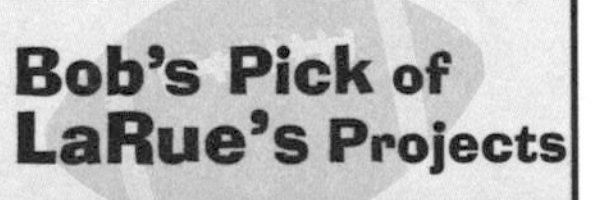

Pick up a copy of LaRue "Transparent." You'll love it.

Three Letters You Need to Read

Here are three testimonies from men who've struggled with sexual temptations and sin, and found hope and even restoration. Their letters remind us of the power of friends, counsel, and most of all, the grace of God. Whether it's a friend or you struggling with one of these issues, I urge you to read these candid, helpful letters.

ON MEN AND ABORTION

HELLO, FRIEND,

Let me tell you about one of the most difficult times in my life. I have two purposes in sharing this: First, so you might not make the same mistake I made, and, second, to let you know about the healing grace of God.

I was an adopted child. When I was twenty years old, I met my birth mother, only to discover that she was seventeen at the time she became pregnant with me, had been beaten by my birthfather, and had parents that wanted her to have an abortion. She chose life and adoption for me in order that I might live and ultimately have the best life I could. The family that adopted me was Christian and they led me to the saving grace of Jesus Christ, and made me feel special for being adopted.

As a Christian, and two years after meeting my birthmother and discovering what she went through to give me life, I found myself experiencing a similar dilemma. I was participating in a relationship that involved promiscuity,

which lead to an unplanned pregnancy. My response was similar to the response of many men after hearing the news; it was silence. My silence was out of shock and denial.

I went home thinking through everything and praying about what to do. I recognized that I was in the relationship for the wrong reasons, because I was not thinking about marriage. I knew that getting married just for the sake of the baby was not a healthy choice. Since I was adopted, I thought adoption for our child might work.

When I got back together with her to talk about the situation, she informed me that she was interested in obtaining an abortion. Since I saw the pregnancy as a problem, I did not fight for this child. I took her to the clinic and paid to have our child killed through an abortion procedure. Driving around waiting for her to be done was the longest period of my life. Most of me was numb, except for my stomach, which was turning over and over. At times, I wanted to turn around and go back and get her. I don't remember where I drove to, but I remember parking somewhere and silently crying and grieving. I knew this was wrong, and I just wished it wasn't happening.

Aborting my child is my life's biggest regret. It is something you never forget, and there is not a day that goes by that I do not wish that my decision had been different.

I went home after dropping her at her apartment, and the shame and guilt put me on my knees begging God to forgive me. The relationship began to deteriorate and not much later ended. The pain from the abortion was unbearable, and I quickly turned to another promiscuous relationship to medicate the hurt. As another form of medication, I turned to athletics where I excelled at just about any sport I tried. But my competitiveness and desire to win often came at the expense of others.

Oddly enough, my healing began in a college philosophy class where I would debate how awful abortion was. In this class, I recognized that I needed healing. God created men to be protectors and providers for their families. Abortion goes directly against those roles, and I had failed at being part of who God had designed me to be. I felt guilty and ashamed.

Society says that pregnancy and abortion are women's issues. Society debates whether there are problems associated with abortion. The truth is simple: Abortion is not just a woman's issue, and there are problems—hurt, loss, shame, guilt, depression, and addictive behaviors. If you are someone who is hurting from a past abortion, there is hope.

First off, you and I are not alone. According to the Alan Guttmacher Institute, there is an average of [Much higher than that!] 4,400 abortions each year. Each one of these abortions involved a male partner in some fashion. You may have been someone who encouraged her to abort, supported whatever decision she made, or someone who even tried to stop her from obtaining an abortion. Either way, a past abortion experience may be affecting you.

Society is wrong. Pregnancy and abortion are not "just a woman's issue." Recognizing this allowed me to grieve the loss of my child. Grieving this loss was a true step towards healing. Receiving forgiveness from Jesus brought me closer to reconciliation. When I read Psalm 103:12, I discovered that when I give my transgressions to God, He removes them from me as far as the east is from the west. I knew He had taken my sin of abortion and removed it completely.

Along with grieving the loss of your child, it is important to confess the role you play in the abortion and/or the role you didn't play. The second part was myself. I did not want the abortion, but my sin occurred when I failed to protect and provide for my child. Sydna Masse of Ramah International points out the biblical significance of confession by noting James 5:16, which says, "Confess your sins to each other . . . so that you may be healed."

It is important to tell someone that you are hurting. Sharing your testimony with someone provides them with the opportunity to come alongside and help carry your burden, Galatians 6:2. Exposing this part of my life was one of the most frightening things I have ever done, but the reward and healing that would follow made it worth my while. Pregnancy Resource Centers (post-abortion support groups) are one of the safest places to initially share this part of your life. Call America's Crisis Pregnancy Helpline toll free and confidentially at 1(800) 672-2296, and a counselor can help you find the center in your area.

I knew that having premarital sex was wrong, but it turned out to cost me much more than my convictions. The most effective way to protect and provide for your family is to abstain from sex until you enter into a committed relationship through marriage. I regret having to tell the woman I married, that I was not a virgin. This part of your being is a special gift and it should be saved to be given to the perfect woman—your wife.

I hope and pray that if you have participated in an abortion, that you will experience a healing journey that leads to the peace that is available through Christ Jesus. Abortion is never the "right" solution. Never encourage or suggest that a friend choose an abortion for their circumstances, no matter how bad it may seem. If you know someone that is hurting because of a past abortion, please help them get connected to someone who can help them.

In His Service for Life,
Brad

Brad Imler, Ph.D. is the Executive Director of America's Crisis Pregnancy Helpline (ACPH). ACPH is a national hotline (http://thehelpline.org) that empowers women and families experiencing unplanned pregnancies or hurting from a past abortion by providing counseling, education, and referrals to resources within their geographical area. He has conducted training for Ramah International, Focus on the Family, and Heartbeat International. He has helped people who are post-abortive through a national call-in counseling show with Dr. Frank Minirth.

ON HOMOSEXUALITY

Hey Guys,

First off, I would like to commend you for reading a book on sexual purity. There are few things in life that affect us as much as our own sexuality. Secondly, my story may be different from yours or it may sound painfully familiar, but I want you to hear that God is bigger than sin and that He works ALL things together for good for those who love Him.

As a third generation Southern Baptist, I accepted Christ at age six and remember being at church every time the doors were open. I loved the Lord, but as I was growing up I began having feelings that made me question whether the Lord loved me. See, an older boy molested me at age nine. And, since I'd heard repeatedly that God was going to judge homosexuals by sending them to hell, you can imagine my utter despair thinking I was now gay. Somewhat of a momma's boy anyway, I began hearing the names "sissy," "queer," and "fag" hurled at me. As I took an inner look and surveyed my actions and feelings, I decided that those who had labeled me must be right. Yet, I wondered in horror at what this would mean for me. Obviously my family, friends, and church wouldn't accept me. Worst of all, I had heard that God couldn't love a homosexual and therefore I was destined for hell.

It was in that time of adolescence that I began the ritual of praying and pleading with God to forgive me and change me. I let Him know at every opportunity how disgusted I felt with myself and how ashamed I was of my very being. I knew I Corinthians 6:9–10 outlined my fate ("nor homosexuals . . . will inherit the kingdom of God"), but I prayed for God's mercy. The more time that passed, the more my feelings intensified and self-hatred grew. Inner conflict plagued my middle and high school years. I kept my thoughts and feelings hidden at all costs.

In January 1990, one month prior to turning eighteen, I attended a Dawson McAllister youth conference. There, Dawson shared that God loves homosexuals and that there was hope for them. Not only did he refer to the familiar

I Corinthians 6:9–10, but he read verse 11 which says "And such *were* some of you" (NKJV, italics added). Yes, God does say that homosexuals won't inherit the kingdom of God along with gossips, liars, adulterers and others. But He also says that change is possible—inevitable with Jesus as the focus. Dawson's ability to look past my problems to me the person changed my life.

In spite of God's calling and revelation, I chose to pursue homosexuality the following year. I chose to be involved in sexual relationships, addictions and to trust in other things more than I did in the Lord. But, His love was unfailing, forgiving, and pursuant of me.

On Easter Sunday, 1991, the Lord spoke to me in a gay bar where I was seeking acceptance and refuge. He said, "Alan, if you choose to stay here the rest of your life, that is, if you choose to live your life as a homosexual, I will still love you. My love and acceptance are unconditional. But what you think is good is the enemy of My best. Trust Me and I will give you My best." I left the bar that evening with the help of two Christian friends who'd happened to drive by, see my car, and hear God tell them to go in and get me. He heard my cry and answered me tangibly. That night I made a choice. I never returned to gay life.

Today, I live in freedom from shame, guilt, and fear of exposure. I am no longer concerned with an eternity in hell. However, I didn't *feel* God's grace, love and forgiveness the minute I decided to abandon homosexuality. Freedom comes as I choose to *know* that these things are mine regardless of how I feel. It is a lifelong journey.

If you are struggling with homosexuality, you may be wondering how in the world you got that way. Are you born gay? Many say homosexuality is genetic, acceptable, an equal alternative, and even a gift from God. None of that is the truth. While these explanations may sound appealing to your heart and mind that's craving an end to the shame and guilt, believing God created you gay isn't the way to find acceptance from Him. He loves you, gay or straight. He wants to be in relationship with you and yet He doesn't want to leave you where you are.

Male homosexuality is an intensely irrational longing to be loved, accepted, and affirmed by another man. It stems from your feelings of inequality to other guys. Homosexual behavior is an illegitimate way to get a legitimate need met. God created us with the core needs, but He meant for them to be met in the proper father-son relationship, later, through boyhood friendships and in ongoing maturing male-to-male adult relationships. In early childhood if the proper development is interrupted, the needs remain and at puberty we begin experiencing "crushes" or "attractions" and we fear that we're gay. Don't be so quick to label or judge yourself. Too many others will rush to that conclusion for you. Rather, choose to take a deeper look. Choose to understand yourself and your circumstances. Choose to open up to a trusted Christian adult who will help you sort through those feelings and get you the help you need.

God loves you no matter what. He died for you. He doesn't expect perfection or for you to get all cleaned up in order to be acceptable. The only qualification for His love is that you realize that you are unqualified and need His help. If you were perfect you wouldn't need a Savior.

Take it from me, God will do amazing things in you if you trust Him and give Him time. Today, I am not perfect. But, I am not a homosexual in action, thought, or identity. I am a husband to my wife, a counselor and mentor to guys struggling with their sexual identity, and a pursuer of God and the truth. I know that all things are possible for you.

I Love You, Man!
Alan Chambers

Alan serves as a staff pastor at Calvary Assembly of God in Orlando, Florida, where his ministry outreach is to high school aged guys struggling with homosexuality. He is a national speaker having appeared on such notable programs, as ABC's 20/20 and The Rikki Lake Show. He is also a member of the board of directors of Exodus International, North America, the worldwide coalition of ministries offering help for those affected by homosexuality. He married his best friend, Leslie, in 1998. They reside in College Park, Florida. Please contact Alan via E-mail at AlanChambers@calvaryorlando.org or by calling 407/644-1199.

ON SEXUAL ADDICTION

This letter wasn't exactly written directly to you. It was a letter Focus on the Family's Dr. James Dobson wrote to a parent. I think it captures very well the significant issues related to masturbation. Perhaps the best part of it is how Dr. Dobson lets us into a private conversation with he and his father—a conversation that each of us should be blessed to have with our dads. I hope you find some answers here.

A PARENT WRITES TO DR. DOBSON: My thirteen-year-old son is in the full bloom of adolescence. I'm suspicious that he may be masturbating when he's alone, but I don't quite know how to approach him about it. Should I be concerned, and if so, what should I say to him?

DR. DOBSON RESPONDS: I don't think you should invade that private world at all unless there are unique circumstances that lead you to do so. I offer that advice while acknowledging that masturbation is a highly controversial subject and Christian leaders differ widely in their perspective on it. I will answer your question but hope you understand that some Bible scholars will disagree emphatically with what I will say.

First, let's consider masturbation from a medical perspective. We can say without fear of contradiction that there is no scientific evidence to indicate that this act is harmful to the body. Despite terrifying warnings given to young people historically, it does not cause blindness, weakness, mental retardation, or any other physical problem. If it did, the entire male population and about half of females would be blind, weak, simpleminded, and sick. Between 95 and 98 percent of all boys engage in this practice—and the rest have been known to lie. It is as close to being a universal behavior as is likely to occur. A lesser but still significant percentage of girls also engage in what was once called "self-gratification."

As for the emotional consequences of masturbation, only four circumstances should give us cause for concern. The first is when it is associated with oppressive guilt from which the individual can't escape. That guilt has the potential to do considerable psychological and spiritual damage. Boys and girls who labor under divine condemnation can gradually become convinced that God couldn't love them. They promise a thousand times with great sincerity never again to commit this despicable act. Then a week or two passes, or perhaps several months. Eventually, the hormonal pressure accumulates until nearly every waking moment reverberates with sexual desire. Finally, in a moment (and I do mean a moment) of weakness, it happens again. What then, dear friend? Tell me what a young person says to God after he or she has just broken the one thousand first solemn promise to Him? I am convinced that some teenagers have thrown over their faith because of their inability to please God at this point of masturbation.

The second circumstance in which masturbation might have harmful implications is when it becomes extremely obsessive. That is more likely to occur when it has been understood by the individual to be "forbidden fruit." I believe the best way to prevent that kind of obsessive response is for adults not to emphasize or condemn it. Regardless of what you do, you will not stop the practice of masturbation in your teenagers. That is a certainty. You'll just drive it underground—or under covers. Nothing works as a "cure." Cold showers, lots of exercise, many activities, and awesome threats are ineffective. Attempting to suppress this act is one campaign that is destined to fail—so why wage it?

The third situation around which we should be concerned is when the young person becomes addicted to pornographic material. The kind of obscenity available to teenagers today has the capacity to grab and hold a boy for the rest of his life. Parents will want to intervene if there is evidence that their son or daughter is heading down that well-worn path.

The fourth concern about masturbation refers not to adolescents but to us as adults. This habit has the capacity to follow us into marriage and become a substitution for healthy sexual relations between husband and wife. This, I believe, is what the apostle Paul meant when he instructed us not to "deprive" one another as marital partners: "Do no deprive each other except by mutual consent and for a time, so that you may devote yourselves to prayer. Then come together again so that Satan will not tempt you because of your lack of self-control" (I Corinthians 7:5).

As for the spiritual implications of masturbation, I will have to defer to the theologians for a more definitive response. It is interesting to me, however, that Scripture does not address this subject except for a single reference in the Old Testament to a man named Onan. He interrupted sexual intercourse with his sister-in-law and allowed his semen to fall on the ground to keep from producing offspring for his brother, which was his "duty" (Genesis 38:8). Though that verse is often cited as evidence of God's disapproval of masturbation, the context doesn't seem to fit.

So, what should parents say to their kids about his subject? My advice is to say nothing after puberty has occurred. You will only cause embarrassment and discomfort. For those who are younger, it would be wise to include the subject of masturbation in the "Preparing for Adolescence" conversation I have recommended on other occasions. I would suggest that parents talk to their twelve- or thirteen-year-old-boys, especially, in the same general way my mother and father discussed this subject with me. We were riding in the car, and my dad said, "Jim, when I was a boy, I worried so much about masturbation. It really became a scary thing for me because I thought God was condemning me for what I couldn't help. So I'm telling you now that I hope you don't feel the need to engage it this act when you reach the teen years, but if you do, you shouldn't be concerned about it. I don't believe it has much to do with your relationship with God."

What a kind thing my father did for me that night in the car. He was a very conservative minister who never compromised his standards of morality to the day of his death. He stood like a rock for biblical principles and commandments. Yet he cared enough about me to lift from my shoulders the burden of guilt that nearly destroyed some of my friends in the church. This kind of "reasonable" faith taught to me by my parents is one of the primary reasons I never felt it necessary to rebel against parental authority or defy God.

Well, those are my views, for what they are worth. I know my recommendations will be inflammatory to some people. If you are one of them, please forgive me. I can only offer the best advice of which I'm capable. I pray that in this instance, I am right.

Dr. Dobson *is founder and president of Focus on the Family. This letter is taken from James C. Dobson, Solid Answers (Wheaton Ill: Tyndale, 1997).*

Letters and inquiries
can be sent to Bob Gresh at
bob@purefreedom.org

or by writing to
Kay Barker
Pure Freedom
360 Lightner Street
State College, PA 16801
814.234.6072

Moody Press,
a ministry of
Moody Bible Institute,
is designed for education,
evangelization,
and edification.
If we may assist you in
knowing more about
Christ and the
Christian life, please write
us without obligation:
Moody Press, c/o MLM,
Chicago, Illinois 60610.

Seven Secrets To Sexual Purity - for women

And The Bride Wore White

Youth are bombarded by worldly messages about sex and love. Without God's help, remaining sexually pure is nearly impossible. Dannah Gresh's book *And the Bride Wore White* exposes our culture's lies about sex, and prepares young women and girls for the world's pressures.

ISBN# 0-8024-8330-5

Seven Secrets to Sexual Purity - Leader's Guide

Based on the book *And The Bride Wore White,* the leader's guide provides practical "how-to" skills for aggressively developing and maintaining purity in an impure world. The guide can be presented in a two-day seminar, one-night sleepover, or a ten-week Bible study.

ISBN# 0-8024-8333-X